flip
your
classroom

REACH EVERY STUDENT
IN EVERY CLASS
EVERY DAY

T0282942

REVISED EDITION

Jonathan Bergmann and Aaron Sams

International Society for Technology in Education
PORTLAND, OREGON • ARLINGTON, VIRGINIA

Association for Supervision and Curriculum Development
ARLINGTON, VIRGINIA

Flip Your Classroom
Reach Every Student in Every Class Every Day
Jonathan Bergmann and Aaron Sams

© 2023 International Society for Technology in Education

Senior Acquisitions Editor: *Valerie Witte*
Copy Editor: *Linda Laflamme*
Proofreader: *Lisa Hein*
Indexer: *Valerie Haynes Perry*
Book Design and Production: *Kim McGovern*
Cover Design: *Beth DeWilde*

Library of Congress Cataloging-in-Publication Data

Names: Bergmann, Jonathan, author. | Sams, Aaron, author.
Title: Flip your classroom: Reach every student in every class every day
  / Jonathan Bergmann and Aaron Sams.
Description: Revised edition. | Portland, Oregon : International
  Society for Technology in Education, [2023] | Includes
  bibliographical references and index.
Identifiers: LCCN 2023008824 (print) | LCCN 2023008825 (ebook) |
  ISBN 9781564849861 (paperback) | ISBN 9781564849878 (epub) |
  ISBN 9781564849885 (pdf)
Subjects: LCSH: Video tapes in education. | Individualized instruction.
  | Teachers—Time management. | Homework.
Classification: LCC LB1044.75 .B47 2023 (print) | LCC LB1044.75
  (ebook) | DDC 371.33/52—dc23/eng/20230301
LC record available at https://lccn.loc.gov/2023008824
LC ebook record available at https://lccn.loc.gov/2023008825

Revised Edition
ISBN: 978-1-56484-986-1
Ebook version available
Printed in the United States of America

ISTE® is a registered trademark of the International Society for
Technology in Education.

ASCD® is a registered trademark of the Association for Supervision
and Curriculum Development. ASCD® product # 323067

About ISTE Books

The International Society for Technology in Education (ISTE) is the leading publisher of books focused on technology in education. Our books and jump start guides promote revolutionary ideas and leading-edge practices that empower learning and teaching in a connected world. They cover a range of edtech topics and tie effective teaching and leadership strategies directly to the ISTE Standards, providing clear, practical guidance to help educators meet the Standards.

About ASCD Books

ASCD empowers educators to achieve excellence in learning, teaching, and leading so that each child is healthy, safe, engaged, supported, and challenged. Our books and quick reference guides feature a diversity of seasoned educators and new voices from all areas of the education community on both time-honored and timely topics like classroom management, instructional strategies, leadership, equity, and social-emotional learning. Our publications allow educators to chart their own learning journey so that they and their students can grow and flourish.

Related Titles

In-Class Flip: A Student-Centered Approach to Differentiated Learning
　　Martha A. Ramírez and Carolina R. Buitrago

The Mastery Learning Handbook: A Competency-Based Approach to Student Achievement
　　Jonathan Bergmann

Flipped Learning: Gateway to Student Engagement
　　Jonathan Bergmann and Aaron Sams

To see all books available from ISTE, please visit iste.org/books.

To see all books available from ASCD, please visit ascd.org/books.

About the Authors

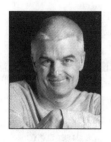

Jonathan Bergmann (@jonbergmann) teaches science and assists with staff development at Houston Christian High School in Houston, Texas. In 2002, Bergmann received the Presidential Award for Excellence for Math and Science Teaching, and he was a semifinalist for Colorado Teacher of the Year in 2010. As one of the pioneers of the flipped classroom, he has helped schools, universities, organizations, and governments worldwide introduce active and flipped learning into their contexts. He's a frequent keynote speaker who challenges and inspires audiences with stories and real-life examples from his classroom. He also serves on the advisory board for TED Education. Bergmann has written or co-authored several books that have been translated into 13 languages, including the landmark ISTE/ASCD book *Flip Your Classroom* and *The Mastery Learning Handbook*, a practical guide to help educators make the shift to mastery learning.

Aaron Sams (@chemicalsams) is an assistant professor of education at Saint Vincent College in Pennsylvania. He's a former high school chemistry teacher, and during that time, he chaired the committee to revise the Colorado science education standards. Sams received the Presidential Award for Excellence in Math and Science Teaching in 2009. He's the co-author of several books, including the landmark ISTE/ASCD book *Flip Your Classroom*, and he regularly publishes his research on STEM education policy and practice. Sams resides in Pittsburgh with his wife and three children, and can often be found biking on local trails, climbing sandstone crags in West Virginia, or cooking in his backyard.

Acknowledgments

We would like to acknowledge all the educators who adopted the flipped model of teaching who supported us on this journey and who helped us continue to refine our ideas. The community of educators that rallied around flipping will always be our tribe, and we are eternally grateful for your friendship and collegiality.

Dedication

For our wives, Kelsey Sams and Kris Bergmann.

Contents

Contents

about the revised edition

We purposely kept the original edition of this book short, hoping you would read it in one sitting or over a weekend at most. We have kept the core of the book (our story) in place for this revision, but have made several updates to the resources and coverage of recent developments since the original edition published. Note that there are instances throughout the book where we mention Jonathan's current school or classroom. Those are recent examples that have been added to this edition, as our education journeys have taken us both beyond the Colorado school where we originally taught as a team.

We have also added some brand-new elements and sections to go a bit deeper into how to successfully implement flipped learning.

New Content

Chapter 8, "Flipped Learning in Action," is a new chapter that features two case studies. One illustrates how an individual teacher applied flipped learning, and the other shows how flipped learning was adopted across an entire school district.

In addition, Appendix A, "Best Practices for Making Quality Educational Videos," is brand new. It focuses specifically on tips to help you create videos for your classes.

Connections to the ISTE Standards

The book provides connections to the Educators section of the ISTE Standards by sharing real-world examples and quotes from a variety of ISTE Certified Educators, representing multiple grade levels and specialties.

Educator
Standards

The **ISTE Standards for Educators** are designed to help teachers help students become empowered learners. These standards will deepen your practice, promote collaboration with peers, challenge you to rethink traditional approaches, and prepare students to drive their own learning.

Quotes from Educators

As we did throughout the first edition, we have again interspersed anecdotes and thoughts from many educators across the globe who have in some fashion flipped their classrooms. One thing that has been reinforced at every stage of our flipped classroom journey is that we can all learn from each other.

foreword

The book you are now reading incited a revolution in education when the first edition was released over a decade ago. Like many revolutions, it started small.

Jonathan Bergmann and Aaron Sams, two rank-and-file chemistry teachers in a Colorado public high school, were simply trying to cope with a basic issue: student absences. Eventually, they came up with the idea of putting classroom lectures on video, so if a student missed class it would be easy to catch up. Soon, they realized they had devised an entirely new way to conceptualize classroom instruction: Remove lecture from class time and put it on video, where it's more useful, and use the liberated time in class for active learning. Thus, flipped learning was born.

The full origin story is in Chapter 1, and I won't spoil it. But suffice to say that the concept grew legs with astonishing speed. Soon, teachers across Colorado, and then all over the US and beyond, were flocking to this idea.

I was late to the party. In 2009, I was designing a new course at my college that needed more time for active learning than its one-credit-hour status would allow. I complained to a colleague that lecture was the problem—it was eating up all the time! My colleague asked me if I'd ever heard of the flipped classroom. I had not; but I soon did. Flipped learning was a perfect fit for my class (though my first attempt was far from perfect). And so I joined the revolution too.

Many pundits at the time panned flipped learning as a fad or a buzzword. But today, it's clear that it has stood the test of time and is more crucial now than ever. The COVID-19 pandemic exposed all the pain points of traditional instruction. We know today about the superiority of active learning over traditional lecture. We also know that students' patience with lecture has evaporated. Young people want to do meaningful things, and sitting and listening to someone talk is not a good use of their time.

All the vectors point toward the same conclusion: We need to make as much time and space as possible in class for active learning. Flipped learning provides the means of doing so. And this book is your guide.

In it, you will find clear explanations of flipped learning, practical steps for implementing it in your class (including explicit connections to ISTE standards), and most importantly: stories, not only the authors' own but also those of others through relatable case studies. Evidence from educational research is useful and important, and there is plenty of it that supports flipped learning. But in the end, what we all need to try anything new to us is someone else's story.

Successful revolutions tend to succeed when the tools for change are put into the hands of everyday people. In this fine new edition of their book, Bergmann and Sams have once again done just this.

Robert Talbert, Ph.D.
Professor of Mathematics, Grand Valley State University

Author, *Flipped Learning: A Guide for Higher Education Faculty and Grading for Growth*

http://Rtalbert.org

CHAPTER **1**

our story:
creating the
flipped classroom

Enrique is struggling in school, specifically in his math course. Every day his teacher stands in front of the class and teaches to the state standards. She uses the latest technology. She received a grant for an interactive whiteboard that is supposed to engage all kids and get them excited about learning. Enrique's problem is that the teacher talks too fast for him, and he can't take notes quickly enough. When he does get all the notes from class onto paper, he doesn't understand what they mean. When he goes home to complete his homework, he continues to struggle because what he wrote down in class during the lecture doesn't seem to match with what he is supposed to do on his assignment. So, Enrique, a hard-working student, has few options: He can go into class early and ask his teacher for help, he can call a friend with the hope that they understood what she said, he can copy the homework from a friend, or he might simply give up.

Janice is active in volleyball, basketball, and track at Eastside High School. She is a conscientious student who always wants to do her best. Unfortunately, she has a difficult science class the last period of every day. She must often leave school early to travel to games and matches, and she misses a lot of classes. She tries to keep up with her science class, but she just can't because she misses so much of it. She sometimes comes in and meets with her teacher before school, but he is often too busy to individually teach her everything she missed.

Ashley has spent the better part of her life learning how to "play school." She is 10 years into mastering the art of meeting her teachers' requirements by making sure that she meets every detail of a grading rubric. She never actually retains the key concepts, despite consistently earning As and Bs in her classes—not because she has demonstrated understanding, but because she has met the requirements in the rubric. Those grades do not accurately reflect what she has actually learned. Ashley is being served very poorly by her school.

Sadly, these scenarios are not uncommon. Many struggling students who genuinely want to learn fall behind instead. Others are so busy that they miss out on key concepts. Still others learn how to "play" school, but never really learn important objectives in their courses. And recently, because of interruptions due to the COVID-19 pandemic, educators around the world have been working frantically to help their students get back on track.

The flipped classroom can address the needs of students such as Enrique, Janice, and Ashley by allowing their teachers to personalize the students' education. You can do the same. This book will show you how!

A Note on Terminology

Before we proceed with our story, we would be remiss if we didn't mention a few important facts:

- We did not lecture exclusively in our classes before flipping; we have always included inquiry-based learning and projects.

- We were not the first educators to use prerecorded videos as an instructional tool, but we were early adopters and outspoken proponents of them. For us, the flipped class would not have been possible without the videos. However, there are teachers who use many of the concepts you will read about in this book and who call their classrooms flipped, but do not use videos as instructional tools.

- We did not come up with the term "flipped classroom." No one owns that term. Soon after the publication of the first edition we had people who advised us to copyright the terms "flipped class" and "flipped learning." To that, we said a resounding "No!" We wanted the concept and term to be in the wild and to grow organically, and that is exactly what happened. We didn't even coin the term. University professor J. W. Baker (2016) claims to have done so in the late 1990s when using VHS tapes from his university library to teach the material in his courses. Daniel Pink (2010) also made an early reference to flipping in a blog post about math education. In addition, Lage, Platt, and Treglia (2000) did early work delivering pre-class content through Microsoft PowerPoint around what they called "inverted classrooms."

As an additional note, in the original version of this book we refer exclusively to the "flipped classroom." Since that time, we also helped popularize the term "flipped learning." In fact, our subsequent book was called *Flipped Learning*. Although an argument could be made that these two terms are distinct, in the ensuing years "flipped classroom" and "flipped learning" have essentially become synonymous. So, regardless of which term you see in this book, you can assume we are referring to the same principle of flipping the time and space in which direct instruction takes place.

Background

In 2006, we both started teaching at Woodland Park High School in Woodland Park, Colorado. Jonathan came from Denver, and Aaron from southern California. We became the chemistry department at our school of 950 students. As our friendship developed, we realized that we had very similar philosophies of education. To make our lives easier, we began planning our chemistry lessons together, and to save time we divided up much of the work. Aaron would set up one lab, and Jonathan the next. Aaron would write the first test, and Jonathan the next.

A problem we noticed right away about teaching in a relatively rural school is that many students missed a great deal of school because of sports and activities. The "nearby" schools are not nearby. Students spent an inordinate amount of time on buses traveling to and from events. Thus, students missed our classes and struggled to stay caught up.

And then one day our world changed. Aaron was thumbing through a technology magazine and showed Jonathan an article about some software that would record a Microsoft PowerPoint slideshow, including voice and any annotations, and then convert the recording into a video file that could be easily distributed online. YouTube was just getting started, and the world of online video was in its infancy. But as we discussed the potential of such software, we realized that this might be a way to keep our students who missed class from missing out on learning. So, in the spring of 2007, we began to record our live lessons using screen capture software. We posted our lectures online so our students could access them.

In all honesty, we recorded our lessons out of selfishness. We were spending inordinate amounts of time reteaching lessons to students who missed class, and the recorded lectures became our first line of defense. The conversation usually went something like this:

Student: "Mr. Sams, I was gone last class. What did I miss?"

Mr. Sams: "I tell you what, go to my website, watch the video I posted, and come see me with any questions you have."

Student: "Okay."

Our absent students loved the recorded lectures. Students who missed class were able to learn what they had missed. Some students who were in class and heard the live lecture began to rewatch the videos. Some would watch them when reviewing for exams. And we loved it because we didn't have to spend hours after school, at lunch, or during our planning time getting kids caught up.

We never could have expected the side effects of posting our lessons online. Because our videos were available online, students and teachers from all over the world began thanking us for them. Students just like ours who had struggled with chemistry found our videos and started using them to learn. We participate in several online science teacher forums, and we began to share the links to the recorded lectures there. Teachers from all over the country began to take notice. Chemistry teachers began to use our video lectures as plans for substitute teachers, and some new teachers used them to learn chemistry content so they could teach it to their students. All in all, it was amazing to see what we were doing in our small town being noticed across the country.

The Flipped Classroom Is Born

In our combined total of more than half a century of teaching, we have been frustrated with students not being able to translate content from our lectures into useful information that would allow them to complete their homework. Then, one day, Aaron had an insight that would change our world. It was one simple observation: "The time when students really need me physically present is when they get stuck and need my individual help. They don't need me there in the room with them to lecture them and give them content; they can receive content on their own."

He then asked this question: "What if we prerecorded *all* of our lectures, students viewed the video as 'homework,' and then we used the entire class period to help students with the concepts they don't understand?"

With this question, our flipped classroom was born. We made a commitment during the 2007–08 school year to prerecord all of our chemistry and Advanced Placement (AP) Chemistry lectures. To make things easier on us, one of us would do unit one of chemistry and the other unit one of AP Chemistry. Then we switched off for each subsequent unit. This meant many early mornings for Jonathan, the morning person, and many late nights for Aaron, the night person in our duo.

Our students are on a block schedule, so we see them for 95 minutes every other day. Every other night our students watch one of our videos as homework and take notes on what they learned. Teaching science courses, we continued to conduct the same laboratory experiments that we had always done. We found that we had more time for both the labs and the problem work time. In fact, for the first time in either of our careers, we ran out of things for the students to do. They were completing all their work with 20 minutes left in class. Clearly, this model was more efficient than lecturing and assigning homework.

We also decided to give the same end-of-unit tests as we had done the previous year. We discuss the details in the next chapter, but, in short, our students learned more and we had some rough data that seemed to indicate the flipped classroom was a better model than the traditional approach.

We implemented the flipped model for one year, and we were very pleased with how our students were learning. We had evidence our model worked and was better for kids. So you would think we would perfect this model and continue to teach that way—but you'd be partially wrong. More on that in a bit.

How Flipping Aids Personalization

Flipping the classroom establishes a framework that ensures students receive a personalized education tailored to their individual needs. Remember Enrique, Janice, and Ashley from our opening story? They represent the struggling students, the over-scheduled students, and the students who get by with superficial learning. Educators are expected to find a way to reach these students with their very different needs. Personalization of education has been proposed as a solution.

ISTE STANDARD IN ACTION

Designer (2.5.a)

Students don't all learn at the same pace or in the same way, and personalizing learning can be difficult—but not impossible. There are ways to reach children through their learning process with just some minor changes. I teach over 100 students on a daily basis. All of my classes are at different learning levels. Something that I've been able to do with the use of technology is provide the content in different ways for my students. My lessons are on slides and I use Nearpod for students to be able to visualize those slides on their 1:1 devices. Through these lessons I provide a variety of lessons to check for student understanding. When it comes time to assess, I've created choice boards using a variety of technology tools that allow the student to select the option or options they feel are most appropriate for their level.

—SAMANTHA MENDENHALL, 7TH AND 8TH GRADE SCIENCE
TEACHER, PORT ALLEN MIDDLE SCHOOL, PORT ALLEN, LA

The movement toward personalization has much merit, but for a single teacher to personalize education for 150 students is difficult and does not work in the traditional educational setting. The present model of education reflects the age in which it was designed: the Industrial Revolution. Students are educated in an assembly line to make their standardized education efficient. They are asked to sit in nice neat rows, listen to an "expert" expound on a subject, and recall the learned information on an exam. Yet somehow, in this climate, all students are expected to receive the same education. The weakness of the traditional approach is this: Not all students come to class prepared to learn. Some lack adequate background for the material, are uninterested in the subject, or have simply been disenchanted with the present educational model.

 Since doing a flipped classroom, I went from not having enough time to get through all the learning to having more than enough time, so that I can now do more hands-on learning, enrichment projects, as well as work more with small groups and implement effective feedback. The flipped classroom has changed my classroom environment, with 100% engagement and students wanting to learn!"

—Jena Sagendorf, 3rd Grade Teacher, Desert
Horizon Elementary School, Phoenix, AZ

For the better part of two decades, educators have been told to provide a personalized education for each student, and most educators believe that personalization is a positive goal to reach for each student. However, the logistics of personalizing 150 different educations each day seems insurmountable to most teachers. Exactly how can a teacher personalize the education of so many kids? How can she ensure that every student learns when there are so many standards to cover? Personalization is truly overwhelming for most educators, and they end up taking the shotgun approach to teaching: Present as much content as they can in the time they have, and hope that it hits as many students as possible—and sticks.

When we began flipping our classrooms, we quickly realized that we had stumbled on a framework that enabled teachers to effectively personalize the education of each student—the goal of educators since the concept of individualized learning first appeared. As we have presented our flipped classroom model to educators around the world, many have said, "This is reproducible, scalable, customizable, and easy for teachers to wrap their minds around."

You may also have noticed some similarities between a flipped classroom and other educational models such as blended learning, reverse instruction, inverted classroom, and 24/7 classroom. All of these models have similar features and could possibly be interchangeable in certain contexts.

ISTE STANDARD IN ACTION

Designer (2.5.a)

The reality that current educators face is that not all students come to us prepared to learn. So, how can we address this when we have 30 students at a time? I love to use flexible groups for this. I try to have different lessons and experiences available for students based on what they need that day. A formative assessment at the beginning or end of class prepares me to place students in differentiated groups based on how well they are doing with the content. Some students might be almost at mastery but need a little more practice. They can watch asynchronous videos to do a lab or activity or take notes based on an article and explain the concepts to a partner. This frees me up to pull small groups for extension or reinforcement, and even meet with individual students for conferencing. The ability to use technology and flipped learning also allows students to have a choice in how they access content. Using the flipped model to enhance a choice board or playlist allows me to offer students podcasts, videos, articles, or hands-on activities in addition to their normal classwork.

—MORIAH WALKER, CYBERSECURITY EDUCATOR, LAKOTA LOCAL SCHOOLS, LIBERTY TOWNSHIP, OH

The Flipped Classroom Grows

As we began this journey, we had no idea that what we were doing was going to spread beyond our four walls. Then, out of the blue, we got an email from a neighboring school district wanting us to come and tell them about the flipped model. They even offered to pay us! So we packed our bags and spent a day in Cañon City, Colorado. You've probably sat in staff development training where the principal or superintendent has brought in some "expert": someone from out of town with a slideshow. Well, we were those experts. When we started, most of the teachers were sitting with glazed expressions, as if they were daring these two yahoos from down the road to capture their attention.

As we shared our story, their slumped bodies began to become straighter. Soon the teachers in the audience were asking questions and showing genuine interest in the flipped model. And then as we broke them into groups to begin practicing how to make their own videos, we realized we had stumbled on something that was much bigger than ourselves. One seasoned teacher told us that in 26 years of teaching, our presentation and workshop was the most valuable professional development day he had ever attended. We suspected his comment had more to do with the simplicity and reproducibility of the flipped model than with our presentation skills.

A few weeks later, our assistant principal came into our rooms and asked us, were we expecting anybody from Channel 11? Much to our surprise, the education reporter from one of the local news stations had heard about us and just showed up on our doorstep. He made a short news clip about what we were doing...and, as they say, the rest is history. We were invited to speak at conferences and asked to train educators at schools, districts, and even colleges. We spoke about the flipped class-room across the United States, Canada, Asia, the Middle East, South America, and Europe.

The Flipped-Mastery Class Begins

Then, one day, our world was rocked by conversations with some of our students. At the end of every year we give students a comprehensive project. In this project, they are asked to analyze a household substance and chemically determine some quantitative property of that substance. The year we implemented the flipped model, students were supposed to analyze Pepsi and determine the percentage of phosphoric acid in the beverage. We have done this project for years, and we were expecting that this group of students, the first who had learned in the flipped model, would set a new standard for good results. When students finish this project, each group has to submit to an oral interview with the teacher. In that interview, we ask some key conceptual questions that get to the heart of what students should have learned in chemistry. We were surprised and disappointed to find that, although this group of students had performed better on tests than students in the past, some of their responses in the interview made it seem that they had learned just for the test, instead of really mastering the essential concepts all chemistry students should learn.

On further reflection, we determined that despite our best efforts to meet the needs of all students, we were still pushing our kids through our curriculum whether they were ready to move on or not. We began to wonder if we could set up a flipped classroom that also had elements of a mastery-learning environment in which students learn a series of objectives at their own pace (Bloom, 1971). Our conversation went something like this: In the traditional flipped model (it feels strange to say that there is a "traditional" flipped model!), all students watch the same video on the same night. Then, in class, all students complete the same activity or lab. But now that we have a library of instructional videos, why does every student need to be on the same topic at the same time?

Another thing that got us thinking about the flipped-mastery model was the entrance of a foreign exchange student into

Jonathan's class. The counselors came to Jonathan and asked him if a student could join his chemistry class at the beginning of second semester. When Jonathan asked about her previous chemistry class, he was told that she had no background. Before we made our videos, there would have been no way to allow such a student into class in the middle of the year. As Jonathan thought it through, he realized that he had a whole library of videos made for chemistry. She could work through them at her own pace. He took the student into his class. She started at unit 1 and worked her way through the chemistry curriculum. In our course we have 10 units that cover the entire year. She got through 8 of the 10 in one semester. As we observed her work, we began to think about a system where all students worked through the material as they mastered the content at their own pace.

 ## ISTE STANDARD IN ACTION

Designer (2.5.a)

To honor that all students learn in different ways, I like to create learning pathways or choice boards that incorporate multiple means of content delivery. For example, one of our learning goals has been for third graders to learn about the continents. The learning choice board provides them with audio, video, and digital book resources to learn about each continent. Students can choose which means works best for them. In addition, the graphic organizer students use to gather their learning provides them with a variety of ways to express their new learning. This could be done by drawing a picture or writing words. Flipping learning like this is very powerful because not only does it give students a personalized learning experience where they are making choices for their learning, but it also gives the teacher time for students who need additional support or extension.

—SARA SCHOEPKE, INSTRUCTIONAL TECHNOLOGY & LIBRARY MEDIA COORDINATOR, WATERFORD GRADED SCHOOL DISTRICT, WATERFORD, WI

Our ultimate goal is for all students to really learn chemistry. We wondered if we could set up a system in which students progress through the course as they master the material. You must understand that we had never been trained in how to implement a mastery system of learning. Subsequently, we discovered that mastery learning has been around for a long time. A great deal of research has been done on how to implement such a system. We didn't consult the literature, we didn't do any research: We simply jumped in.

Our first year of teaching with the flipped-mastery model was a year with a high learning curve. We made a lot of mistakes. When that year was over, we looked at each other and asked, "Should we continue with this?" Yet both of us realized that we could not go back. We had seen our students learning chemistry more deeply than ever before, and we were convinced. Our method was changing students' abilities to become self-directed learners.

The Flipped Classroom Explodes

Since publishing the first edition of this book in 2012, we have been humbled by the growth of the flipped classroom around the world. For a time, we both crisscrossed the globe working with teachers, schools, and ministries of education helping them implement the model. We worked with small groups of teachers and keynoted at conferences with as many as 25,000 people in attendance.

Early criticism of this book was both the lack of research around flipped learning and the fact that the book didn't cite any references. Certainly, some of that was on us as we sought to tell the story of our classes and what had worked for *us*. In this edition, we tried to remedy that shortcoming. It has helped that since 2012 the number of research articles about flipped learning has exponentially increased. Thousands of peer-reviewed papers have been written, and the vast majority of them have demonstrated the efficacy of flipped learning. Research into flipped learning has proven that it works in virtually any subject, level, or country. In fact, the first edition of this book has been cited more than 8,000 times in research articles around flipped learning.

Here is a very brief selection of some studies showing the contexts in which flipped learning can work:

- Harvard Medical School has flipped (Fu, 2015).

- Flipped learning has helped train dental hygienists (Kim, 2020).

- A study out of Iowa State University concluded that flipping is promising for laboratory courses, because coming "ready to participate in the laboratory activities allows students to spend more time enhancing their skills and techniques" (Anderson, Franke, & Franke, 2017).

- Researchers in South Korea studied if flipped learning increased higher order thinking of preservice teachers. Their study was unique as they tracked student questions and categorized them using Bloom's Taxonomy. They found that the quality of student questions was enhanced by flipped learning. This study is also interesting because they flipped the training of preservice teachers, which can only bode well for future teachers in South Korea (Heo & Chun, 2018).

- Researchers in Thailand are developing a model that connects flipped learning with constructivist philosophy and critical thinking. They propose that connecting these three strategies will enhance student learning (Jantakoon & Piriyasurawong, 2018).

- Martin H. Malin and Deborah I. Ginsberg (Chicago-Kent College of Law) have successfully used a flipped class approach for four years for their law school students (Malin & Ginsberg, 2018).

- Researchers at Brigham Young University studied the effect of flipping a large lecture-hall statistics class and found "significant improvement in the students' performance and course satisfaction with the flipped classroom. Overall, the results showed that the flipped classroom model can be used in large lecture classes with the help of undergraduate teaching assistants and the use of additional labs" (Nielsen, Bean, & Larsen, 2018).

- A thesis from Hong Kong used a systemic meta-analysis of flipped learning research in K–12 and tertiary science. It found that flipped learning shows a significant increase in student achievement (Zhang, 2018).

- A study in the Philippines found that flipped learning reduces math anxiety in junior high students. This study illustrates how the additional time provided by flipped learning to build student–teacher relationships helps students cope with difficult concepts (Segumpan & Tan, 2018).

- A metanalysis examined 73 studies on flipped learning and found that the most cited advantage to flipped learning was increased student performance. It also noted that the most challenging aspect of implementing flipped learning is getting students to do the pre-class work (Akçayır & Akçayır, 2018).

Little did we know that flipped learning would take on such a pivotal role in helping teachers teach through the COVID-19 pandemic. Every teacher we knew who had successfully flipped their classes (and between us we know a lot of teachers) was tapped by their administration to help their peers navigate the quagmire of remote and hybrid learning. Though flipped learning is not remote learning, nor is it online learning, many of the same principles and tools have enough overlap that they helped teachers during the pandemic. One teacher even tweeted that flipped learning teachers had been preparing for the pandemic for ten years.

The post-pandemic need and commitment of teachers has been the driving force behind the change in my classrooms to adopt a flipped learning methodology. We teachers have internalized that teaching and learning with flipped learning is no longer a complementary option. It is the option."

—Carmen Llorente Cejudo, Teacher of Educational Technology Degree in Pedagogy, Faculty of Education, University of Seville, Spain

Are You Ready to Flip?

If you have made it this far, you realize that we have a pretty high tolerance for change. We are willing to try almost anything if we think it will help our students. And fortunately, we have made many good decisions along the journey. We have also made many mistakes. It is our hope that if you decide to implement the flipped or even the flipped-mastery model, you will learn from our mistakes and improve on our model.

We also hope that as you read, you realize that there is no single way to flip your classroom. There is no such thing as *the* flipped classroom. There is no specific methodology to be replicated, no checklist to follow that leads to guaranteed results. Flipping the classroom is more about a mindset: redirecting attention away from the teacher and putting attention on the learner and the learning. Every teacher who has chosen to flip does so differently. In fact, even though we developed our flipped class together and are next door to each other, Jonathan's classroom still looks different from Aaron's classroom, and our personalities and individual teaching styles shine through the commonalities.

CHAPTER **2**

the
flipped classroom

At this point you should have an idea of what a flipped class entails, but you may be asking exactly what in the classroom is "flipped." Basically, the concept of a flipped class is this: That which is traditionally done in class is now done at home, and that which is traditionally done as homework is now completed in class. Another way of thinking about it is "flipping" the direct instruction to be completed by the individual learner and reserving class time for the application of the content. But as you will see, there is more to a flipped classroom than this.

The Flipped Classroom Structure

Day in the Life
of a Flipped
Classroom

We are often asked about what the flipped classroom looks like on a day-to-day basis. (Scan the QR code to view a video that provides a brief overview.) Essentially, we start each class with a few minutes of discussion about the video from the night before. One of the drawbacks to the flipped model is that students cannot ask immediate questions that come to their mind, as they could if the topic were being taught "live." To address this issue, we spend a considerable amount of time at the beginning of the year training the students to view our videos effectively. We encourage them to turn off phones and other distractions while they watch the video. We then teach them that they now have the ability to "pause" and "rewind" their teacher. We encourage them to liberally use the pause button so they can write down key points of the lesson.

Cornell Note-
taking System

In addition, we instruct them in the Cornell note-taking system, in which they take notes, record any questions they have, and summarize their learning. (Scan the QR code to learn more about this system.) Alternately, some teachers choose to provide a note-taking guide in which students fill in various blanks as they view the instructional video. Students who adopt these models of note-taking typically come to class with appropriate questions that help us address their misconceptions. Communities that have 1:1 initiatives and ubiquitous access to Wi-Fi outside the school may choose to use digital tools to encourage note-taking. Some teachers in such schools even embed their videos in online applications in which questions can be embedded to prompt students to immediately respond to what they just learned. Teachers can use responses to these questions or student notes to evaluate the effectiveness of instructional videos. If every student has a similar question, we clearly did not teach that topic well, and we make a note to remake or correct that particular video in the future.

ISTE STANDARD IN ACTION

Designer (2.5.a)

When I initially started to flip my classroom, I quickly realized that students didn't inherently understand how to watch videos to learn content. Creating videos for students to learn anytime, anywhere allows students to personalize their learning, but, as we started this shift in practice, I needed to teach students how to learn independently. The first few instructional videos we watched together in class. I modeled note-taking with a think-aloud to demonstrate when I felt I needed to pause and replay a section of the video. I modeled how to turn on closed captions and use some of the other playback tools.

Students come to us with different needs. Some benefit from using sketchnotes, while others find outlines to be helpful. By using class time to watch our first flipped lesson together, we could talk about note-taking strategies, which allowed my learners to reflect on their individual needs. This helped students to feel more confident that they were using their time productively.

—APRIL BURTON, INSTRUCTIONAL TECHNOLOGY CONTENT LEADER, FRANCIS HOWELL SCHOOL DISTRICT, O'FALLON, MO

After the initial questions are answered, students are given the assignment for the day. It might be a lab, an inquiry activity, a directed problem-solving activity, or a test. Because we are on a 95-minute block schedule, students usually do more than one of these activities in any given class period. While students complete the assigned work, we circulate the room and provide individualized assistance and feedback to *every student, in every class, every day.*

We continue to grade assignments, labs, and tests just as we always have under the traditional model. But our role in the classroom has dramatically changed. We are no longer the presenters of information; instead, we take on more of a tutorial role. Since the 1990s, teachers have been encouraged by Alison King (1993) to be the "guide on the side" rather than the "sage on the stage," and a flipped classroom is an excellent way to step into this paradigm. The change experienced by the teacher was probably identified best by Shari Kendrick, a teacher in San Antonio, TX, who adopted the flipped model: "I don't have to go to school and perform five times a day. Instead, I spend my days interacting and helping my students." One huge benefit of flipping is that the students who struggle get the most help. Like Shari, we spend our time walking around the room helping students with concepts they are stuck on.

> *Flipped learning has provided me with an opportunity to build stronger relationships with both students and staff. I am able to personalize instruction much more effectively than ever before. In addition, flipped learning has provided me with an opportunity to reflect on my own teaching practices in order to continue to make improvements in my instruction."*
>
> — Stephanie Quataro, Learner Centered Specialist, Regional School District 13, Durham, CT

In the traditional model, students would usually come into class confused about some of the homework problems from the previous night. Generally, we would spend the first 25 minutes doing a warm-up activity and going over those problems they didn't understand. We would then present new content for 30 to 45 minutes and spend the remainder of the class with independent practice or a lab.

In the flipped model, the time is completely restructured. Students still need to ask questions about the content that has been delivered via video, so we generally answer these questions during the first few minutes of class. This allows us to clear up misconceptions before they are practiced and applied incorrectly. The remainder of the time is used for more extensive hands-on activities and/or directed problem-solving time (see Table 2.1).

TABLE 2.1 Comparison of Class Time in Traditional versus Flipped Classrooms

Traditional Classroom		Flipped Classroom	
Activity	*Time*	*Activity*	*Time*
Warm-up activity	5 min.	Warm-up activity	5 min.
Go over previous night's homework	20 min.	Q&A time on video	10 min.
Lecture new content	30–45 min.	Guided and independent practice and/or lab activity	75 min.
Guided and independent practice and/or lab activity	20–35 min.		

The Teacher's Role in a Flipped Class

Let's look at a typical unit in Aaron's AP Chemistry class and see an example of how the role of the teacher has changed.

Aaron's AP Chemistry class begins the night before in the home of each student. Students are not assigned problems or reading from the book, but rather, a video. Using their preferred device and viewing method, all students will watch a video of Aaron and Jonathan explaining the material that will be applied in class the following day.

Class begins. Aaron quickly takes attendance and starts a question-and-answer session. Students ask questions about the previous night's video, and Aaron helps clarify misconceptions. After 10 minutes or so, Aaron instructs the students to take out their packet of practice problems, many of which are similar in structure to the type of questions they will see on the AP

Chemistry exam. He leads the class through a few examples that reflect the content students learned the night before and takes any further questions. Then it is time to work. The students complete the remaining assigned problems while Aaron moves around the class helping students as they have questions. A solution guide is available to students who want to check their work.

ISTE STANDARD IN ACTION

Citizen (2.3.b)

During the pandemic, our school was lucky enough to support families without internet access with hotspots. Students were all given their 1:1 school devices to use at home (iPads PK–1 and Chromebooks 2–12). When we started back in person, it was important that students still had access to the internet outside of school hours. Many families were able to continue accessing the internet through lower cost plans in our community. The local library had desktops for the community to use. At school, we taught students how to load videos or turn on offline access to files on their 1:1 Chromebooks before they left for the day. Students knew the steps they needed to take to get their work done and many were more comfortable asking for help when they needed it. Teachers were encouraged to load videos on YouTube so that students could access them easily from cellular devices. In a recent community survey, approximately 94% of parents surveyed reported having internet access at home. Shifting the mindsets of parents, students, and teachers has created a community that helps each other be successful.

—LANCY COLLINS, INSTRUCTIONAL COACH FOR TECHNOLOGY, PK–12, HOMER CENTRAL SCHOOLS, HOMER, NY

On days when a lab will be conducted, no video is assigned. Instead, students complete a pre-lab activity at home. In class, Aaron fields any pertinent questions about the lab and discusses safety. Then the students begin experimenting. Under a traditional model, the completion of any calculations and discussions is usually assigned as homework after a lab. Under the flipped classroom model, however, the next video is assigned for homework, and students are given time in class the next day to complete the lab. This allows Aaron to answer specific questions about the lab and assist struggling students with their calculations, as well as discuss the data collected as a class.

When exam day rolls around, all students take the exam at the same time and are provided timely feedback so misconceptions can be addressed. Ultimately, all students need to be through the curriculum by the end of April so preparation can be made for the AP exam in May. So that all students are prepared for the exam by the established date, they all work at the same pace.

> " Since I have adopted the flipped learning approach, I have seen a tremendous increase in not only student engagement, but student passion. If an educator can find a way to ignite passion and curiosity in a student, then the engagement piece will follow. Flipped learning has been transformational in creating active and effective learning in all of my classes!"
>
> —Joy de los Reyes, Felician University, School of Business & Information Science, Rutherford, NJ

Clearly, the class is centered around the students and not the teacher. Students are responsible for viewing the videos and asking appropriate questions. The teacher is simply there to provide expert feedback. The students are responsible for completing and sharing their work. Because a solution guide is available, students are motivated to learn, not just to complete the assignments in a rote manner. Students are responsible for making appropriate use of the resident expert to help them understand the concepts. The role of the teacher in the classroom is to help students, not to deliver information.

ISTE STANDARD IN ACTION

Facilitator (2.6.a)

The flexibility and freedom within flipped classrooms allow students to take ownership of learning goals and outcomes. The example given in this chapter focuses on AP Chemistry students working together with a solution guide to check their understanding. Structuring a class to allow for teacher facilitation of content and letting students move on when concepts are mastered fosters a sense of wanting to learn, rather than just checking boxes.

I often use locked modules within our learning management system (Canvas) that have self checks, partner checks, and teacher checks. These checkpoints force students to work at a pace that is comfortable for them, but also require students to take control of their own learning. The checkpoints also give me plenty of formative assessment data that I can use to guide my activities, small groups, and student needs. This freedom for students not only strengthens their content knowledge but also their awareness of any weaknesses they have. And, it encourages willingness to seek help when needed from both peers and teachers, a skill they will need in whatever field they pursue.

—MORIAH WALKER, CYBERSECURITY EDUCATOR,
LAKOTA LOCAL SCHOOLS, LIBERTY TOWNSHIP, OH

CHAPTER 3

the case for
flipping
your classroom

Flipping the classroom has transformed our teaching practice. We no longer stand in front of our students and talk at them for 30 to 60 minutes at a time. This radical change has allowed us to take on a different role with our students. Both of us taught for many years using a lecture format. We were both good teachers. In fact, Jonathan received the Presidential Award for Excellence in Math and Science Teaching as a lecturer, and Aaron received the same award under the flipped model. As we look back, however, we could never go back to teaching in the traditional manner.

Case for
Flipped
Learning

The flipped classroom has not just changed our own classrooms. Teachers from around the world have adopted the model and are using it to teach Spanish, science, and math to elementary, middle, and high school students, as well as adults. We have seen many examples of how flipping a classroom can change kids' lives. It can change your students' lives too. In this chapter, we want to highlight why you should consider flipping your classroom. (Scan the QR code for a video that presents a case for flipped learning.)

Flipping speaks the language of today's students

Today's students grew up with ubiquitous internet access. Despite any misgivings we may have about social media, it is hard to imagine a world without it. Our students are immersed in it. The 2012 edition of this book referred to YouTube, Facebook, and MySpace as the social media *de jour*. Now, just a decade later, MySpace is history, replaced by Instagram, Twitter, Snapchat, TikTok, and a host of other social media platforms that will inevitably become outdated and replaced at some point themselves. Regardless of the platforms available, students can typically be found doing their homework while texting their friends, messaging on some other messaging app, video chatting with another friend, and listening to music all at the same time. Many of our students report that when they come to school, they have to turn off and dumb down because their schools ban cell phones, laptops, and any other digital devices. The sad thing is that most students are carrying in their pockets a more powerful computing device than the vast majority of computers in our underfunded schools—and we don't allow them to use it!

When we present the flipped classroom to educators, we usually get an *ooh-ahh* reaction from our audiences, which are primarily made up of adults who did not grow up with the always-on digital world. When we began flipping, we were surprised at our students' lack of amazement. After about two weeks of watching the videos, they had settled into learning, and the "wow" factor was gone. These students understand digital learning. To them, all we are doing is speaking their language. Don't get us wrong: We are not saying they don't appreciate learning this way, but because nearly every social media and learning platform now supports video content, instruction via video is not a big deal for today's students.

One concern we have heard from adults is that by flipping a classroom, teachers are increasing screen time in front of a device, which aggravates the disconnect many adults feel with today's youth. To that we say that we are infiltrating the video/digital culture instead of fighting it. We believe educators should embrace digital learning and use it to help our students learn, instead of telling them they can't learn with today's tools. It seems preposterous to us that some schools still have not embraced this change.

When you walk into our classrooms, you will see students engaged in a variety of activities using various digital devices. Students work on our (obsolete) class computers, they use their smartphones, they work together, they work independently, they experiment, and they interact with their teacher. We encourage our

Bad Reasons for Flipping Your Classroom

Because some guys who got a book published told you to.
We're flattered that you are interested in what we have to say, but do not adopt any teaching strategy without thinking it through first.

Because you think it will create a digital age classroom.
Pedagogy should always drive technology, never the other way around.

Because you think you will become cutting edge.
Flipping does not necessarily use the latest technology, and as we write this revised edition, it has become fairly mainstream.

Because you think flipping your classroom exempts you from being a good teacher.
Teaching is much more than good content delivery. In fact, a flipped classroom can expose poor teaching quite quickly.

Because you think it will make your job easier.
Flipping will not make your job any easier, but it may make it more rewarding.

students to bring in their own electronic equipment because, frankly, it's better than our school's antiquated technology. To that effect, we also encourage schools that do not have a 1:1 initiative to embrace a BYOD policy.

Flipping helps busy students

Students today are busy, busy, busy. Many are overprogrammed, going from one event to the next. Our students appreciate the flexibility of the flipped classroom. Because the main content is delivered via online videos, students can choose to work ahead. Jonathan had a student who was a competitive gymnast who regularly traveled to out-of-state competitions. When she was gone, she missed most of the instruction in her classes. But because she was in a flipped classroom for science, she didn't miss any of the content in that class. She chose to work ahead when competitions were coming up. When she returned, she had at least one class she didn't have to worry about.

Aaron had a student who was heavily involved in student council. When homecoming was approaching, she worked ahead and got one week ahead in his class. When homecoming week happened, she used Aaron's class time to work on homecoming activities. These two students not only learned how to "work the system"; they also learned valuable life lessons in managing their time. This would not work in a traditional classroom, but flipping the classroom provides a great deal of flexibility to help students with their busy lives.

Flipping helps struggling students

When we taught in the traditional manner, the students who tended to get most of our attention were the best and brightest—students who would raise their hands first and ask great questions. In the meantime, the rest of the students would passively listen to the conversation we had with the inquisitive students. But since our introduction of the flipped model, our role has changed. In the flipped model, we spend most of our class walking around to help the students who struggle most. We think this may be the single most important reason students thrive in the flipped model. This is not to say that we ignore our top students. But the majority of our attention no longer goes to them. Now it is directed to the students who need the most help.

Flipping helps students of all abilities to excel

Our special education teachers love this model as well. Because all the direct instruction is recorded, students with special needs can watch the videos as many times as they need to learn the material. No more frantically trying to copy down notes with the hope that they'll understand them later. Instead, students can pause their teacher, rewind their teacher, and make sure they actually learn the important concepts.

Flipping allows students to pause and rewind their teacher

As educators, we usually have a specific curriculum and standards we need to cover in our courses. Students are expected to learn a given body of knowledge, and most of the time we hope that they understand our presentations of the content. However, even the best presenters and lecturers have students who fall behind and do not understand or learn all that is required. When we flipped the classroom, we gave our students control of the remote. Giving students the ability to pause their teachers is truly revolutionary.

Jonathan's daughter was once in his class, and while Jonathan observed her watching one of the videos at home, she suddenly burst out and said, "I love these videos." He asked her why. She said, "I can pause you!"

Pausing is a powerful feature for a number of reasons. Making students all sit in tidy rows and listen to their teacher eloquently explain his or her area of expertise is not always an effective means of communicating to them. Lectures often move too fast for some students and too slowly for others. Quick learners understand immediately and get bored waiting, while struggling students take more time to process. Inevitably, when the teacher clicks the arrow to move to the next slide, a small group of students calls out in protest, asking to go back to the previous slide. When we give students the ability to pause their teachers, they have the chance to process at the speed that is appropriate for them. In our classes, we especially encourage students who process more slowly to use the rewind button while watching our videos so they can hear us explain something more than one time. If they still don't understand, we work with them individually or in small groups in the classroom.

On the other end, students who are often bored because the teacher is going too slowly appreciate the pause function for different reasons. In our classes, these typically are our busiest students, involved in a myriad of activities and sports. Giving them the ability to pause helps these students with time management. Jonathan's daughter was one of these students, and she liked the pause button so she could break up the lesson into shorter segments and learn on her own schedule. We even have had a few students who watch our videos at double speed. These students are able to process our instruction faster than most, and they find this to be a better use of their time (even though our voices sound as if we've been inhaling helium).

These examples are not to say that a well-crafted lecture is necessarily bad. But that well-crafted lecture with the power of being able to be paused and reviewed under the control of the learner becomes an even more powerful learning tool. We often conduct mini-lectures with groups of students who are struggling with the same content. The beauty of these mini-lectures is we are delivering "just-in-time" instruction when the students are ready for learning.

Flipping increases student–teacher interaction

A statement we frequently hear goes something like this: "This is a great method for online teaching, but I don't want to replace my classroom with online courses." Though flipping certainly has great potential to change online education, the purpose of this book is not to promote the benefits of such education. We are both classroom teachers who see our students every day. Most students today still come to a brick-and-mortar school where they see both their teachers and their peers.

Blended Learning Models

We believe that flipping allows teachers to leverage technology to increase interaction with students. We must be clear, however. We are not advocating the replacement of classrooms and classroom teachers with online instruction. In fact, we strongly believe that flipping the classroom creates an ideal merger of online and face-to-face instruction known as a "blended" classroom. The Clayton Christensen Institute at Harvard University, one of the leading resources on blended learning, have categorized a flipped classroom as a subset of blended learning (2023). (Scan the QR code to learn more.)

Teachers play a vital role in the lives of their students. They are mentors, friends, neighbors, and experts. Having face-to-face interaction with teachers is an invaluable experience for students.

ISTE STANDARD IN ACTION

Designer (2.5.a)

Flipping the classroom will never replace the need for the support and guidance of a good teacher, but technology can help the teacher better meet the needs of all students in many different ways. In my blended class, which meets half online and half in person, I use the learning management system's modules to house the course learning materials such as readings and videos; then I require my students to complete an online quiz to assess their understanding of the material. I make sure to include both readings and videos and sometimes audio files such as podcasts to accommodate learner differences. The online quizzes are short, formative assessments that are untimed and allow for multiple attempts to obtain mastery. Having students independently struggle a bit with the content before coming to class helps them better retain it, so later in class they are better able to retrieve the content during our class discussions. I use a combination of multiple-choice questions and short-answer responses to reach both lower and higher order thinking.

—MADELINE CRAIG, ED.D. ASSOCIATE PROFESSOR, SCHOOL OF EDUCATION AND HUMAN SERVICES, MOLLOY UNIVERSITY, NY

Flipping allows teachers to know their students better

We as teachers are not only at school to teach content, but also to inspire, encourage, listen, and provide a vision for our students. This happens in the context of relationships. We have always believed that a good teacher builds relationships with students. Students need positive adult role models in their lives. We hope we can be such role models. We developed these relationships before we flipped the classroom, but flipping allows us to build better relationships with our students because of the increased student–teacher interaction.

The year we started flipping, we encouraged students to interact with online messaging after school hours. Most of the time the content of these messages was (and still is) along the lines of "How do I get help on problem X?" or "What is the benchmark for this coming week?" Because we make the instructional videos together, most of our students do not think of Jonathan or Aaron as their teacher. They think of *us* as their teachers. Thus, some students connect better with Aaron, and some better with Jonathan. One day that first year, one of Aaron's students started messaging Jonathan, and at first, the messages were all about science. Soon the tone of the messages changed. Jonathan realized this student was calling out for help and referred him to our counseling staff. As it turned out, this student had been kicked out of his house and was going through some intense personal issues. Although flipping did not create this relationship, it helped create a positive environment where the struggling student could interact with an adult, and this student got the help he needed.

Flipping increases student–student interaction

One of the greatest benefits of flipping is that overall interaction increases: student to teacher and student to student. Because the role of the teacher has changed from presenter of content to learning coach, we spend our time talking to kids. We answer questions, work with small groups, and guide the learning of each student individually. When students are working on an assignment and we notice that several of them are struggling with the same thing, we spontaneously organize these students into a tutorial group.

Because the role of the teacher has changed to more of a coach than a deliverer of content, we have the privilege of observing as students interact with each other. As we roam around the class, we notice the students developing their own collaborative groups. Students help each other learn instead of relying on the teacher as the sole disseminator of knowledge. It truly is magical to observe. We are often in awe of how well our students work together and learn from each other.

Some might ask how we developed a culture of learning. We think the key is for students to identify learning as their goal, instead of striving for the completion of assignments. We have purposely tried to make our classes places where students carry out meaningful activities instead of completing busywork. When we respect our students in this way, they usually respond. They begin to realize—and for some it takes time—that we are here to guide them in their learning instead of being authoritative pedagogues. Our goal is for them to be the best learners possible and to truly understand the content in our classes. When our students grasp the concept that we are on their side, they respond by doing their best.

Flipping allows for real differentiation

One of the struggles in today's schools is accommodating a vast range of abilities in each class. We have everything from students who excel, to average students, to students who struggle with our content, to students who cannot read. Flipping the class showed us just how needy many of our students were and how powerful the flipped classroom is in reaching students all along this broad range of abilities.

Because the majority of our time is used to walk around the room and help students, we can personalize the learning of all. For our students who quickly understand the content, we have found that if they can prove to us their understanding of a particular objective, we will cut down on the number of problems they need to do. Think of these as individual contracts with each student, where the student has to prove understanding. Students appreciate this because they realize we are not interested in busywork, but rather learning.

For our students who struggle, we look for key understanding. We realize that our course is hard for many students and that learning doesn't come easily for all. For these students, we often modify their work on the fly by asking them to complete only key problems instead all of them. This way our students who struggle will learn the essential objectives and not get bogged down with some of the more advanced topics that usually just confuse them.

ISTE STANDARD IN ACTION

Facilitator (2.6.a)

One of the strengths of flipping instruction is that the ownership of the learning process is shifted to the student and the teacher is free to support and engage with individual students or groups of students who are actively learning. This shift not only allows students to learn in ways that are best suited for them, but students are also more engaged in their learning. When I am supporting classroom learning, I gather a variety of resources for students to use to learn content aligned with the specific learning goal. This provides students with choice in what type of materials they will use and what direction their learning will take. This choice proves very empowering for most learners. I am able to have conversations with individual students that need assistance or redirection. What I usually see, when learning is delivered this way, is that students want to continue learning and that the learning goes deeper than if I delivered the content to the whole class.

—SARA SCHOEPKE, INSTRUCTIONAL TECHNOLOGY & LIBRARY MEDIA COORDINATOR, WATERFORD GRADED SCHOOL DISTRICT, WATERFORD, WI

Flipping changes classroom discipline

Under a traditional model of teaching, we had students who consistently did not pay attention in class. These students were often a distraction to the rest of the class and negatively affected everybody else's learning. They were often either bored or just simply unruly. When we flipped the classroom, we discovered something amazing. Because we weren't just standing and talking at kids, many of the classroom discipline problems evaporated. Students who needed an audience no longer had one. Because class time is primarily used for students to either do hands-on activities or work in small groups, those students who were typically a distraction became a nonissue. They either did not have an audience or they were no longer bored and were willing to dive into the learning.

Don't get us wrong. We still have to redirect students. We still have students who underperform. But so many of the bigger classroom discipline issues have simply disappeared.

> **"** Including a flipped learning approach in my language classes has allowed my students to develop autonomy, become more responsible for their own learning, and grow in confidence. Recording short videos to teach grammar through storytelling has seen more engagement with the language and has had a positive effect on teacher–student rapport and student–student rapport through in-class follow-up activities."
>
> —Lisa Wood, EFL Teacher (English as a Foreign Language), Colegio Estudio, Madrid, Spain

Flipping changes the way we talk to parents

We both remember years of sitting in parent conferences, where parents would often ask us how their son or daughter behaved in class. What they were really asking was, "Does my son or daughter sit quietly, act respectfully, raise their hand, and not disturb other students?" These skills are certainly good for all to learn, but when we first started flipping the classroom, we struggled to answer this question.

You see, the question is a nonissue in our classroom. Because students are coming with the primary focus on learning, there are two real questions now: Is each student learning or not? And if not, what can we do to help them learn? These are much more profound questions, and when we discuss them with parents, we move the focus to a place that will help parents understand how their students can become better learners.

There are myriad reasons why a student may not be learning well. The student may have some missing background knowledge. The student may have personal issues that interfere with learning. Or the student may be more concerned with "playing school" than actually learning. When we (the parents and teachers) can diagnose why the child is not learning, we create a powerful moment where the necessary interventions can be implemented.

Flipping educates parents

Another surprising thing happened when we started talking to parents during parent conferences. Many of them told us they loved our videos. We then asked, "You watch our videos?" As it turns out, many of them were watching right alongside their students and learning science. This led to interesting discussions between students and parents about the content of our lessons. This has been echoed across the country as other teachers have adopted our model. They have told us similar stories of educating their parent community.

At a conference we attended a few years ago, one of the keynote speakers was a kindergarten teacher who told us the following story. She taught in an ethnically diverse school that had many new English language learners. One of the key ingredients in becoming a good reader is to be read to. She was awarded a grant for some devices on which she recorded herself and others reading books. The students would then take the devices home with copies of the corresponding book and would listen to the story being read to them.

When students returned the devices, she noticed that often the batteries almost drained. She knew how long the batteries would last and expressed her puzzlement with her students. Then during parent conferences, one mother told her she was sorry for draining the device's batteries. The mother explained that not only was she listening to the stories, but so were the student's grandmother, aunt, and whole extended family. The teacher's recordings were educating many more people than she ever expected.

ISTE STANDARD IN ACTION

Collaborator (2.4.d)

Parents are essential stakeholders and co-collaborators in student learning in our classrooms. Technology can be very useful for communicating with them on a regular basis to make sure they're kept in the loop on classroom happenings. Our students come to us with a variety of learning needs, but their parents also need multiple ways of receiving various information. I use Wakelet to send out a newsletter each week. Parents can easily translate the newsletter, if needed, into a different language. I provide various visuals for information, bulleted details, and sometimes videos to provide parents with all of the information that they may need to understand what is going on in the science classroom. Through the week I provide short snippets and reminders through Remind (text messaging service for educators) to continue to keep them up to date.

—SAMANTHA MENDENHALL, 7TH AND 8TH GRADE SCIENCE TEACHER, PORT ALLEN MIDDLE SCHOOL, PORT ALLEN, LA

Flipping makes your class transparent

In this age when a segment of our communities distrusts the educational establishment, flipping opens the doors to our classrooms and allows the public in. Our videos are posted on the internet, and our students' parents and others have free access to them. Instead of wondering what their students are being exposed to in the classroom, parents can find our lessons just a click away. Although the COVID-19 pandemic exposed some instances where a misalignment existed between teacher's values and a community's values, other communities were pleased to see the care teachers took to ensure that video instruction was clear, respectful, and helpful.

Like it or not, schools are competing for students. Our school loses students to neighboring schools for a variety of reasons. Much of our loss has been because some parents incorrectly perceive our school to be less academic than nearby schools. Posting our videos and opening our instructional practices to the public has brought some of these students back to our school.

Flipping is a great technique for absent teachers

We teach in a semi-rural school where it is hard to obtain qualified substitute teachers. We especially have a hard time getting qualified teachers to walk into a chemistry class. When we first started recording our lessons and posting the videos online, we simply recorded our lessons live in front of our students. It then dawned on us that we could prerecord a lesson for our students when we knew we were going to be gone. Jonathan was headed to a wedding out of town and thought he would try this out. He sat down in front of his computer and recorded the lesson he would normally have given. The substitute plan was simply to turn on the classroom projector, pull up the video file, and press Play. Students took notes as if he were there in class. This way his students didn't miss a beat. They got the same lesson on the right day. Students reported how almost eerie it was to hear Jonathan's voice without him being present in the room.

This method is being used across the country. An elementary teacher in our district, when gone, prerecords his lessons for his students. Doing so ensures that students are taught the way he wants them to be taught, and he does not have to reteach on his return. The substitutes appreciate this method of teaching because students get just what the teacher wants. We even know of science teachers across the country using our videos as the substitute plans when they are gone.

> " Flipping my classroom was a huge change for everyone (including myself), but I will never go back to traditional teaching. Our class time together is so much more productive and personal now, and my students are learning so much better."
>
> —Kara Street, High School Math Teacher, South Knox High School, Vincennes, IN

Flipping can lead to the flipped-mastery program

This chapter has been a bit awkward for us to write because we no longer just flip our classrooms. Instead, we use the flipped-mastery model, in which students move through the material at their own pace. No longer do all students watch the same video on the same night. Students watch and learn in an asynchronous system where they work toward content mastery. We should note that we did not start using the flipped-mastery program until two years after abandoning the traditional model. Our journey has occurred over several years and continues today. We recommend that those interested in flipping make the change gradually.

CHAPTER **4**

how to implement
the flipped classroom

When we talk to teachers about flipping their classrooms—even enthusiastic, motivated teachers—we hear the same two questions over and over: "Where will the videos come from?" and "How will I fill my in-class time?" In this chapter, we address the logistics of implementing a flipped classroom. We'll help you decide whether making your own videos or finding high-quality videos is your best approach, as well as offer a few tips on both. Finally, we share suggestions from teachers in multiple content areas on how to make the most of the extra time your gain in your flipped classroom.

Homework: The Videos

A temptation for teachers new to the flipped classroom is to create a video for everything. When we began this journey in 2007, we really did not have a choice except to create our own content. Needless to say, there is now plenty of high-quality instructional video content available. There is also some not-so-great content out there, however, so buyer (or viewer) beware.

Before jumping into video production, carefully consider whether or not a video is the appropriate instructional tool for your desired educational outcome. If a video is appropriate, then proceed with planning and creating (or finding) one. If a video is not appropriate, then do not make one just for the sake of making a video. Doing so would be a disservice to your students and would be a prime example of "technology for technology's sake." Only employ the technology if it is an appropriate tool for the task at hand. Use your professional judgment, ask your peers and mentors, and even ask your students.

Probably the single most daunting task teachers face when trying to flip their classrooms is accessing or producing high-quality videos. When we make our videos, we sit in our classroom and talk to the computer and each other. This is much more difficult than teaching in front of a live audience. Students are not present, and thus we have to bring a somewhat artificial dynamic presence. We don't want to bore our students with dry videos, so we try to make them interesting. Sometimes it takes a number of tries and a lot of time. If you don't have the time to create your own videos, struggle with technology, or are not comfortable speaking in front of a computer screen, we encourage you to think about using somebody else's videos as you implement a flipped classroom. (If you are already very comfortable both with technology and with recording, on the other hand, you may want to skip ahead to the "Making Your Own Videos" section.)

Using Other Teachers' Videos

Video Playlist

Using videos produced by other teachers rather than recording your own may be your best option as you begin flipping your classroom. If you find a gifted teacher who has already made videos in your subject, by all means, feel free to use them. Some time ago we made our chemistry videos available online. Many chemistry teachers who wanted to flip their classrooms simply used our videos and did not produce their own. Others used our videos for some of the flipped lessons but created their own videos for the rest. (Scan the QR code to check out some of Jonathan's recent videos.) With the explosion of YouTube and other video sharing sites, the number of videos is exponentially growing. Many of these videos can be used in a flipped classroom. It is important to note that you need to exercise care when using others' created resources to avoid copyright violations. Always link to videos rather than downloading and distributing them. Also, if you use any video content that resides behind a paywall, be sure that you have the permission to share them with your students. Always give credit where credit is due, and never distribute videos without the appropriate authority to do so.

The key is to find quality videos regardless of your subject matter. Where do you find good-quality videos? There's not an easy answer. Depending on your subject, you may have to look far and wide. However, the exponential growth of free online video resources is making the search increasingly easier. That said, finding videos that are also aligned to your state and local standards, or even in your language, sometimes may be more difficult than creating your own. There are some amazing YouTube channels with educational video content you can use, but digging through the entirety of YouTube or Vimeo to find just the right fit could be overwhelming. Fortunately, if you don't want to mine those massive video repositories, smaller education-oriented options are available. Table 4.1 offers a few good starting points for teachers to begin their video curation journey.

TABLE 4.1 Recommended Sources for Education Videos

Video Source	Description	QR Code
PBS Learning Media	Resources from PBS, searchable by grade level	
National Geographic Education	Searchable by grade level or topic	
Annenberg Learner	Repository of programming on many topics for education use	
Teachertube	Teacher-created videos for classrooms	
Math TV	Math videos from basic math through calculus	
Schooltube	Teacher-created videos	
Jonathan's YouTube Channel	Jonathan's YouTube channel with science content and flipped learning videos	

Video Source	Description	QR Code
Mr. Wootube Channel	Eddie Woo's (Australian Educator and friend) YouTube channel, a great source of math videos	
Crash Course History	Hank Green's YouTube channel for all things history-related	

Making Your Own Videos

When we talk about recording a video, most teachers think of a video camera on them while they teach their class. Although this might be effective in some cases, we believe there are better ways to make videos for use in the flipped classroom. We have used a variety of methods to create instructional videos, with the most common being screencasting programs, such as Camtasia and Screencastify. Screencasting applications capture anything on your screen, your voice, a small webcam feed of your face, and any digital pen annotations you make. The pen feature is especially useful for lessons that involve mathematical problem-solving. Creating slides ahead of time with a bunch of numbers appearing on a PowerPoint slideshow is not as dynamic as sharing, in real time, what you write with a pen and describing your thought process as you explain a problem. Other features, such as picture-in-picture, video clips, and many other post-production items can be added to improve the quality of the videos.

For more information and tips on video creation, please see the appendix, "Best Practices for Making Quality Educational Videos."

ISTE STANDARD IN ACTION

Designer (2.4.a)

You certainly can't do it all on your own, and it can be over-whelming trying to create video segments for key areas of your content. Flipping provides you with an excellent opportunity to collaborate with your teaching team or other content teachers.

Getting together with colleagues, reviewing how they approached the same content, and trading resources really expanded my thinking and helped me to realize I was not in this by myself! Over time, I collaborated with other content teachers via social media and found another level of approaches and resources to draw from!

—JOHN PADULA, TECHNOLOGY INTEGRATION SPECIALIST,
HOPKINTON, MA

Class Time

Once you've set up your flipped class and made (or chosen) your videos, you will find yourself with extra time, a luxury you probably have never had in your career as a teacher. Many years ago, while we presented at a conference in British Columbia, one young teacher asked what all teachers who flip inevitably ask: "If I use your model, what will I do with my kids each day in class?" She realized that most of her time in class was spent standing in front of the room and talking to her students. If her "talking" was prerecorded, what would she do each day? This led to a great conversation about what kinds of activities would truly engage her students.

Despite the attention that the videos get, the greatest value added to any flipped classroom is the in-class time that every teacher must evaluate and redesign. Because we shifted our direct instruction outside of our classroom, our students over the years have been able to conduct higher quality and more engaging activities. Teachers who adopt the flipped model use the extra time in myriad ways depending on their subject matter, location, and style of teaching. We asked some of our colleagues to share how they have changed their class time. Following are some examples, but we would encourage you to check out our series of subject-specific books for more information (see iste.org/books).

Foreign Language Classes

In foreign language classes, teachers are recording grammar lessons and conversational starters so as to create time in class to use the language more practically. This includes engaging in more conversation, reading literature, and writing stories, all in the target language. We visited one of these classes, a level 1 class, and observed students actively speaking Spanish. They were responding and gesturing in ways that corresponded to the teacher's instructions, which were entirely in Spanish. He would then ask students questions, and they would respond in Spanish. He reported to us how the videos had freed him to do more of these engaging activities in his classroom.

 I was shocked at how much better my students who spoke little to no English did in my classes. I teach a lot of technical concepts in the engineering technology department, and when I started using flipped learning the English learner's grades skyrocketed."

—Jason Hlavacs Ed. D., College Adjunct Professor, Triton College, Melrose Park, IL

Math Classes

Math teachers are finding the time to really help their students engage with deep analysis of mathematical concepts. Others are embracing math manipulatives and emerging technologies where students are engaged not just in learning the algorithmic computation, but also in deeply wrestling with the intricacies of the math concepts. Flipped math classes are becoming laboratories of computational thinking, inquiry, and connectedness with other areas of science, technology, engineering, and mathematics.

Science Classes

POGIL

One concern about the flipped classroom that has been recently posed is whether flipping is compatible with an inquiry approach to teaching science. We and others have responded with a resounding yes. Flipping a science class creates more time and more opportunities to include inquiry learning. In science classes, teachers who flip have time for students to engage in more inquiry-based activities and to conduct more in-depth experiments. In the chemistry education community, POGIL (Process Oriented Guided Inquiry Learning) has become a powerful tool for students to create conceptual understanding without direct instruction (scan the QR code to learn more). The flipped classroom is ideally set up for this type of learning, and we have incorporated many POGIL activities into our classroom. When a well-written POGIL activity is conducted, the students learn all they need to learn via guided inquiry, and there is no need to teach the material with a video. In cases such as this, we use the POGIL activity as the instructional tool in lieu of a video. However, we've found that some students still use our instructional videos as a secondary resource for remediation.

Social Science/Language Arts/Humanities Classes

Social science instructors report using their extra time to discuss current events in light of the previous night's instructional video. Others are finding time to delve deeply into original document analysis. There is more time to debate, give speeches, conduct *pro se* court, and discuss what students are learning more deeply—without having to worry about a robust conversation being interrupted by a bell. There's plenty of time to write, write, write, and even more time to analyze and discuss each other's writing through peer review.

Physical Education Classes

We were surprised to hear that some of the teachers most excited about flipped classrooms were physical education teachers. This dynamic team of teachers realized the flipped class had great potential in their courses. They told us that the most important aspect of the physical education class is for their students to be moving. Physical education teachers reported that they spent too much time teaching students such topics as the rules of games and necessary techniques. By making videos of rules and technique demonstrations, the teachers enabled students to more quickly get moving and participating in the important physical education activities when they arrived at class.

 Flipped learning was for me like 'opening a window in a dark room.' When I learned about this approach, I was already giving up on my career as an educator, because I saw that my students were not learning. By using flipped learning I achieved my goals as an educator and my students achieved their learning objectives."

—Jonathan Da Rocha Silva, Neuroeducator, Higher Education, Group Sura, Colombia

Project-Based Learning

Another concern is whether or not a flipped class is compatible with project-based learning. Again, we cheer yes. We love the idea of discovery-based learning driven by student interest. Most of us do not operate in an environment that allows for this, but educationally speaking, it is enticing and has great benefit. Picture a class driven by student-identified problems or interests: Students are exploring a real-world problem and developing solutions, and then suddenly realize that they need to know how to perform a particular mathematical function in order to execute their solution.

The teacher now faces a decision. Does she spend valuable class time teaching the entire class how to perform the appropriate math and risk boring the advanced student and losing the student who struggles? Or does she create an instructional video (or perhaps access an archived one) to give the students what they need, without sacrificing class time for direct instruction? Marrying the technological tools and asynchronous content delivery used in a flipped classroom with a student-directed approach to deciding what is learned can create an environment in which curiosity thrives. There is no need to spend time reintroducing concepts that are well established and just need to be quickly presented and learned, or to use valuable class time to deliver new content.

Student-Created Content

Flipped classrooms can give students more time to create their own content. Students today have a broad range of ways to create content to demonstrate their understanding of various topics. They can create blogs, videos, podcasts, or many other educational products that help them build on their knowledge. We see great value in student-created content, and these can also be used in subsequent academic years as instructional content.

the
flipped-mastery
classroom

Mastery learning has been around for quite some time. It was first introduced in the 1920s, but it got little attention until the 1960s, when it was popularized by Benjamin Bloom (1971). He likened the present educational institutions to a race where only the fastest runners were rewarded. He argued that almost all students can master any content, given enough time and support. When mastery learning was implemented well, studies showed that nearly 80% of all students could learn all of the important content compared to 20% taught with the traditional model.

The basic idea of mastery learning is for students to learn a series of objectives at their own pace. Instead of all students working on the same topics at the same time, all of them work toward predetermined objectives. Mastery learning is usually done in a course with a discrete body of knowledge in which mastery of one objective is necessary for success in all subsequent objectives.

A Quick Overview of Mastery Learning

The key components of mastery learning are:

- Students work either in small groups or individually at an appropriate pace.

- The teacher formatively assesses students and gauges student understanding.

- Students demonstrate mastery of objectives on summative assessments. For students who do not master a given objective, remediation is provided.

Most of the research on mastery learning shows improvement in student achievement. Other outcomes cited are increased cooperation among students, increased student self-assurance, and students receiving a second chance at demonstrating mastery of a given objective. During the 1970s, mastery learning received a lot of attention, but it has now been largely abandoned in favor of the model seen in most brick-and-mortar schools. Most schools found it too difficult to implement the mastery system. Reasons cited for the difficulty included how often teachers must repeat themselves, how many different assessments must be written, and the difficulty of assessing so many objectives at the same time.

But we've moved on from the 1960s and 1970s. The technology explosion has made many of the difficulties of mastery learning easier to overcome. Essentially what we have done is leverage technology to make mastery possible. Our prerecorded videos have created an environment in which the burden of repetition is placed on the student. No longer is the teacher physically needed to reteach most topics. Students can simply rewatch or more fully engage with the instructional video. The teacher can then spend more quality time physically reteaching the students who most need the additional instruction.

ISTE STANDARD IN ACTION

Analyst (2.7.b)

Flipping a mastery-based classroom has become increasingly easier as technology tools catch up with teacher vision and innovation. Not only are videos readily available for teachers to use and share via YouTube, but video creation can be as simplified or extensive as a teacher wants with tools like Screencastify and WeVideo. However, more important than the product being simple for teachers to use or create, the learning process is also made easier with today's technology. For example, while coaching teachers on best instructional practices I encourage them to use Google Forms for an entrance or exit slip as a grouping strategy. Teachers can ask students to answer questions, complete simple tasks, or to gauge their own understanding of a standard in order to group students in meaningful ways. In addition to Google tools, there are other tools utilized by our district such as Canvas and the mastery paths used within their modules or Nearpod to provide real-time data during a presentation. With these tools, I am able to help teachers find ways to forma- tively assess students and use the data provided to inform their flipped classroom instruction. Once teachers have their known entry point for students on understanding a given standard, they are able to either create or find videos that support students' learning. This allows teachers to provide tools that encourage growth without losing them because the content is too simple or too difficult.

—TIFFANY REXHAUSEN, INNOVATION SPECIALIST, LAKOTA LOCAL
SCHOOLS/LIBERTY JUNIOR SCHOOL, LIBERTY TOWNSHIP, OH

We have also leveraged technology to solve the problem of the numerous exams necessary for a mastery model. All of our assessments are administered using computers. Each student is assessed differently from his classmates, yet the same objectives are assessed. In addition, students get a different version of the exam each time they take it. Available technology makes it much easier to have multiple assessments. The time to grade these assessments is greatly reduced, as well, because most of the questions are graded by the computer. Mountains of unsecured paper exams that must be manually graded are no longer necessary. This section serves as only a brief introduction to the flipped-mastery classroom. For a step-by-step guide on how to implement mastery and competency-based learning in your classroom, consult Jonathan's book *The Mastery Learning Handbook: A Competency-Based Approach to Student Achievement* (2022).

Mastery Class
in Action

What Is a Flipped-Mastery Classroom?

A flipped-mastery classroom takes the principles of mastery learning and marries them with modern technology to make a sustainable, reproducible, and manageable environment for learning. If you were to walk into one of our classrooms, you would see much asynchronous activity—all students working on different activities at different times. Our students would be busy and engaged in their learning. You would see some students conducting experiments or other inquiry activities, some watching videos on their personal or school-issued devices, some working in groups mastering objectives, some interacting at whiteboards or drawing on tables, some studying in small groups, and some taking assessments in the school's learning management system. You would also see some working one-on-one or in a small group with the teacher. (To see this in action, scan the QR code to watch a three-minute video of Jonathan's current classroom.)

> *Using flipped learning in classrooms for over 20 years, I have found that being able to differentiate learning, keeping lessons student-centered, and providing flexibility for my students has been much easier than group activities presented in a traditional teaching environment. Students who need additional time to process material have benefited from having resources available 24/7 and demonstrated a higher level of application in the classroom."*
>
> —Jeff Renard, Founder, Vermont Virtual Learning Cooperative, K–12 Statewide Online School, VT

If you watched us throughout the class, you would observe several things: At the beginning of class we organize our students. We check to see who might need to conduct a lab, who needs to take an exam, and who needs remediation on a particular objective. You would observe us moving around the room interacting with students. We talk to every kid, in every class, every day. If a student or a group of students is ready for an experiment, we spend a few minutes discussing with them the main point of the experiment, the key safety principles, and what they should or should not be looking for. If students are ready for us to show them a science demonstration, we get a group together, demonstrate the principle, and then have a post-demonstration discussion. If students struggle on any one specific objective and need to review, you would see us working with them at a whiteboard, or just in a round-table discussion. If a student struggles to demonstrate mastery of any objectives on the summative assessments, we review his past attempts of the assessment with him and provide him with individualized remediation to ensure his future success. Sometimes, at this point we also provide the struggling student with an alternative form of assessment or allow the student to create his or her own way to demonstrate mastery of the objective.

You might ask how we can do so much with so many kids at the same time. Frankly, this is our struggle. We are constantly moving around the room giving attention to those who need it and making sure that all students are learning what they need when they need it. We have called this our three-ring circus of learning because there are so many different activities happening at the same time. Though as we look at a typical day, it probably should be called a ten-ring circus. Teaching in the flipped-mastery model is tiring, and our minds have to constantly switch between one topic and the next, and from one activity to another.

In order to function as an effective teacher in the flipped-mastery environment, we believe a few characteristics are necessary.

The teacher should be a content master. A teacher who is not proficient in his content area cannot operate in a flipped-mastery class. The ability to mentally move from one topic to another is necessary, and a comprehensive understanding of the interconnectedness of the content is essential.

The teacher must be able to admit when he or she does not know the answer to student questions and must be willing to research an answer with the student. Pride will only slow the teacher down and prove to be a detriment to student learning. The teacher should take these opportunities to demonstrate what it means to be a learner: The teacher is the lead learner in a classroom. Teachers should show students what adults do when they do not know an answer, teach them how to collaborate, and guide them through the vast ocean of information in which we swim in our interconnected world.

The teacher must be able to flow through a class period in a nonlinear fashion. All the students are at different places in their mastery and understanding of the learning objectives, and it is the role of the teacher to meet each student where she or he is. The mastery model hinges entirely on the teacher meeting the student at the point of need, not the student meeting the teacher at the prescribed place in the curriculum.

The teacher must be able to relinquish control of the learning process to the students. This can be hard for many teachers. If you feel you need to be in complete control of everything that happens in your class, then mastery learning won't work for you. There is a certain level of chaos that happens in every mastery classroom that is good because it gives students more ownership of their learning.

ISTE STANDARD IN ACTION

Analyst (2.7.b)

One digital tool that I love to use to flip learning and embed assessments is Quizzizz. Quizzizz allows me to create a lesson with learning slides, videos, pictures, links, etc. and also embed questions to check for student understanding of the content. There are a variety of question types to meet diverse learning needs: multiple choice, fill in the blank, drawing, open ended, audio response, video response, and more.

I also find Google Forms to be another very effective way to assess learning. I have also used the Google extension Mote to add audio capabilities to my forms so that readability is not a barrier when I am assessing student understanding. The Mote extension creates audio links that can be embedded with each area of text within the form. This is especially useful with primary students who are beginning readers. Mote can also be very useful in allowing teachers to share audio directions to guide students in their lessons.

There are many digital tools available today to support teachers and learners in assessment. These are two of my favorites.

—SARA SCHOEPKE, INSTRUCTIONAL TECHNOLOGY & LIBRARY MEDIA COORDINATOR, WATERFORD GRADED SCHOOL DISTRICT, WATERFORD, WI

Components of a Flipped-Mastery Classroom

Flipped mastery sounds tiring, and you might be thinking it is too much work. Let us break this down and identify the key components necessary to make flipped mastery work. There are four main components of a flipped-mastery classroom that must be in place before you start.

First, you must establish clear learning objectives. Objectives are the desired outcomes of learning for each student. Use your state standards, national frameworks, and your best professional judgment to determine what you want your students to know and be able to do.

Second, determine which of these objectives are best achieved through inquiry and which are best learned through direct instruction. Create a video or find a pertinent reading for those objectives that will benefit from direct instruction. You need to have either produced your own videos/texts, or found videos/texts that will teach the content you want in the way you want it taught. Remember, as time goes on, more and more teachers are implementing some sort of a flipped model. Many of these teachers are making their videos available on the internet, so you may or may not need to produce all of your own videos. If producing the videos seems too daunting, find someone else's.

When you have either made or chosen other videos, you now need to make sure your students have access to them. Most teachers post the videos on sites such as YouTube and use video-tracking software such as Edpuzzle (edpuzzle.com), Perusall (perusall.com), and Actively Learn (activelylearn.com). As we have worked with schools around the world, we have found that it is best that schools choose one tool for video interaction and stick with it. It causes too much cognitive load for students if there are too many tool choices. Choosing one tool also simplifies professional development for a school. We talk more about these issues in Chapter 7, which covers the nuts and bolts of the flipped-mastery model.

> In my role as a teacher, flipped learning helped me leverage my in-class learning time in the best possible way by allowing me to focus on the important things (student relationships and questions). In my current role as an administrator, I continue to use the strategies to guide my staff in best practices. Specifically, the use of in-class time to help develop relationships and teach the 'meaty' part of the content."
>
> —Delia Bush, Assistant Principal, Hudsonville High School, Hudsonville, MI

Third, you need to incorporate engaging learning activities to be done in class. We make up a packet for each unit that contains the follow-along notes for the video, all experiments students will be doing, and all of the suggested worksheets.

Fourth, you must create multiple versions of each summative assessment for students to demonstrate their mastery of each learning objective in a particular unit of study. This is most efficiently and effectively done through the use of a test bank on a computer-generated testing system. Virtually every major learning management system has this important feature. Currently Jonathan is using D2L (d2l.com), but you could easily use Moodle (moodle.org), Blackboard (blackboard.com), Schoology Learning (powerschool.com/classroom/schoology-learning), or Canvas (instructure.com/canvas). Similar to which video tool you use, it almost doesn't matter. What matters is that a school uses one and sticks to that tool. (More on this in Chapter 7.)

ISTE STANDARD IN ACTION

Analyst (2.7.b)

A tool I use often in my classroom is Nearpod, and it provides me with so many opportunities to assess or check for understanding in my middle school science classroom. At the beginning of a lesson, I assign a bell ringer that's connected to the previous lesson. This allows me to check to be sure they're maintaining their learning. The questions do vary as well (multiple choice, drag and drop, multiselect, writing, etc.) to ensure students have practice with the question types that they struggle with. During my lesson I provide formative assessment checks that vary in style. Students have the opportunity to answer in a variety of different ways, based on what they're comfortable with giving. Some students type their responses better, and some verbalize better. I do the same at the end of the lesson. I use the objective to create one or two questions to check their understanding. No matter what, I'm able to create multiple ways for them to show understanding of the content through the use of Nearpod.

—SAMANTHA MENDENHALL, 7TH AND 8TH GRADE SCIENCE
TEACHER, PORT ALLEN MIDDLE SCHOOL, PORT ALLEN, LA

At the beginning of each unit packet we have an organizational guide that has a list of objectives, corresponding videos, readings from the textbook, learning activities, and lab activities. This organizational guide is a road map to the unit that guides students through the unit of study and provides them with the appropriate framework and supporting activities to meet each learning objective. Figure 5.1 is a sample of one of these guides, and Figure 5.2 is an example of an organizational guide with a checklist for students to track their progress.

ORGANIZATIONAL GUIDE FOR OBJECTIVES AND ACTIVITIES

ATOMIC-1

Objective: Be able to discuss the history of the atomic theory

Reference: Video1/WSAtomicTheroy1

Text 5.1

Required Activities: Cathode ray tube demo (not in packet—see teacher)

ATOMIC-2

Objective: Be able to determine the number of protons, neutrons, and electrons, and name of an atom

Reference: Video2/WSAtomicTheory2

Text 5.2, 5.3

ATOMIC-3

Objective: Understand atomic mass, isotopes, and average atomic mass

Reference: Video3/WSAtomicTheory3

Text 5.3

Required Activities: Vegium lab

ATOMIC-4

Objective: Understand the basic structure of the periodic table

Reference: Video4/AtomicTheory4

Text 5.4

Required Activities: Annotate Your Periodic Table

ATOMIC-5

Objective: Be able to explain the models of the atom

Reference: Video5/WSAtomicTheory5

Required Activities: Mystery Tube Lab (not in packet—see teacher)

ATOMIC-6

Objective: Explain the current quantum mechanical model of the atom as it relates to electrons

Reference: Video6/WSAtomicTheory6

Text 13.2

Required Activities: WS Atomic Theory-6

ATOMIC-7

Objective: Be able to write electron configurations and orbital notations for electrons for any element

Reference: Video7/WSAtomicTheory7

Text 13.2

ATOMIC-8

Objective: Explain the wave nature of light

Reference: Video8/WSAtomicTheory8

Text 13.3

ATOMIC-9

Objective: Explain how light reveals the "position" of electrons in atoms

Reference: Video9/AtomicTheory9

Text 13.1

Required Activities: Flame test lab, "And Then There Was Light"

ATOMIC-10

Objective: Calculate the wavelength, frequency, energy, and "color" of light

Reference: Video10/WSAtomicTheory10

Text 13.3

ATOMIC-11

Objective: Be able to compare the comparative size of atoms and ions

Reference: Video11/WSAtomicTheory11

Text 14.2

ATOMIC-12

Objective: Compare the ionization energies of different atoms

Reference: Video12/WSAtomicTheory12

Text 14.2

ATOMIC-13

Objective: Compare the electronegativities of different atoms

Reference: Video13/WSAtomicTheory13

Text 14.2

Required Activities: Periodicity Graphing Activity

Figure 5.1 A sample objective and activity organizational guide

	OBJECTIVE	PROOF OF UNDERSTANDING
6.1	What is the mole?	• I watched & took detailed notes on video 6.1 (5 min) • I completed WS 6.1 • I Completed the Penny Lab • I passed Mastery Check
6.2	What is molar mass? Be able to calculate the molar mass of compounds	• I watched & took detailed notes on video 6.2 (8 min) • I completed WS 6.2 • I passed Mastery Check
6.3	Be able to do One-Step Mole Conversions	• I watched & took detailed notes on video 6.3 (10 min) • I completed WS 6.3 • I passed Mastery Check
6.4	Be able to do Multi-Step Problems	• I watched & took detailed notes on video 6.4 (10 min) • I completed WS 6.4 • I completed Mole Lab • I passed Mastery Check
6.5	Understand percent composition and be able to determine the percent composition of compounds	• I watched & took detailed notes on video 6.5 (10 min) • I completed WS 6.5 • I passed Mastery Check
6.6	Given mass or percent, be able to determine the empirical formula of a compound	• I watched & took detailed notes on video 6.6 (10 min) • I completed WS 6.6 • I completed Empirical Formula Lab • I passed Mastery Check
6.7	Given the molar mass of a compound, be able to determine the molecular formula of a compound	• I watched & took detailed notes on video 6.7 (10 min) • I completed WS 6.7 • I passed Mastery Check

Figure 5.2 This sample organizational guide lists each objective, and students can use the second column to check off items as they complete/master them and then present their proofs of understanding to their teacher.

CHAPTER 6

the case for
the flipped-mastery
model

Now that you are familiar with the flipped-mastery model, you may be asking yourself why you should consider implementing the model. It may seem like a lot of effort to set up, and you might not be totally convinced that the model will work in your setting. Most of the reasons we cited in Chapter 3 about why you should use the flipped model apply here as well, but the flipped-mastery model has even more benefits than the flipped model. The flipped-mastery model has completely transformed our classrooms, how we think about education, and how we interact with students. Following is a list of reasons we could never go back to a more traditional model of teaching.

The **mastery model** teaches students to take responsibility for their own learning

When we started developing the flipped-mastery model, we did not realize how it would completely change every aspect of our professional lives. Our classrooms are now laboratories of education where students take responsibility for their own learning. When we taught in a traditional model, students were there just to "sit and get." The students waited for us to tell them what to learn, how to learn it, when to learn it, and how to prove to us they had learned it. For some students this worked, but others just became disengaged and lost.

With the flipped-mastery model, the onus for learning is placed squarely on the students. In order to succeed, the students must take responsibility for their own learning. Some students are being asked for the first time to take ownership of their education. Learning is no longer an imposition on their freedom, but rather a challenge to be unpacked and explored. As the teacher gives up control of the learning process, the students take the reins, and the educational process becomes their own.

At the beginning of one school year, Jonathan had one student who just wanted to sit and get—because it was easy and exactly how she was used to functioning at school. She was physically present at school, but learning usually got in the way of her social life. She just hoped to get by with minimal effort and a C. She might have been able to do this in a more traditional model, but with flipped mastery, she had to demonstrate her understanding to her teacher. During the entire first semester she butted heads with Jonathan. He kept insisting that she learn the concepts. He even caught her cheating a couple of times, but with some discussion, he continued to tell her she had to demonstrate her understanding. Over time, she realized that school was easier and less time-consuming if she made the effort to learn the first time she encountered an assignment. She was capable, but not terribly interested. Around February, she finally decided that learning was worth her time and effort. She chose to make learning a priority. When she grasped this, she began to work ahead by watching videos before they were due, she began to fully engage in the learning process, the questions she asked her teacher about each video got deeper, and overall, she became one of Jonathan's most improved students.

ISTE STANDARD IN ACTION

Facilitator (2.6.a)

As an instructional coach, I've noticed that mastery-based learning often gets a bad rap with teachers. They have so many questions like, "What happens as students get further ahead?" and "How do I manage the class if everyone is going at different paces?" Oddly enough though, going mastery-based in my own classroom probably saved my career since I was at a point of high burnout. Because I was giving students on-the-spot feedback as they completed assignments or activities, my grading became much more manageable. I was no longer taking piles of papers home to grade. My tier 1 intervention also became more manageable as I worked with individuals or small groups in the feedback process to help them understand a concept. When integrating the flipped classroom instructional model with mastery-based learning I am able to duplicate myself, in a way, so that I am free to support students with learning and feedback.

One thing I noticed about my students with mastery-based learning is that they became more invested in their learning. That's because students had some elements of choice, they had more of my personal attention, and they could move at their own pace. Pacing for students is important because if a student understands something quicker than others, they become bored and a potential behavior concern. On the other hand, if they feel rushed in their learning, students will give up or feel defeated quicker, also becoming a potential behavior concern. When they are all highly invested and engaged in the learning process, off-task behaviors are minimized.

—TIFFANY REXHAUSEN, INNOVATION SPECIALIST, LAKOTA LOCAL
    SCHOOLS/LIBERTY JUNIOR SCHOOL, LIBERTY TOWNSHIP, OH

This story is not atypical. At first students wonder "what's up" with this unusual system. But as students begin to embrace it, they begin to develop a mature understanding of the nature of learning, knowledge, and their role in education. Most of our science students will not go on to become scientists, engineers, or doctors—but when we teach them to take responsibility for their own learning, we have taught them one of life's most valuable lessons.

The **mastery model** creates a way to easily personalize and differentiate the classroom

We frankly had no idea what would happen when we started the flipped-mastery model. We didn't read the literature. We didn't do a case study. Nor did we ask for permission from our administration. Because we believed it would be good for our students, we simply jumped in. Little did we realize that we had stumbled on an easy way to personalize and differentiate the classroom for all students.

"Differentiation" is a buzzword in today's educational community. When we talk to teachers around the country, most admit they are not differentiating very well because they are not physically able to meet every student's individual needs. With large classes and limited time, they feel overwhelmed. They admit that they teach to the middle of their class. If they teach their subject too fast, they leave students behind; if they go too slowly, the faster students get bored.

Flipped mastery allows the direct instruction to be asynchronous, so differentiation for each student becomes possible. The pace of the class is appropriate for each student. This personalizes the learning for each student. For example, Rachel, a future engineer, brought her teacher an assignment that she had completed to prove that she had mastered an objective. She was one of our top students who planned to eventually attend a competitive college and change the world of engineering. If there was even the slightest mistake in her work, we would send her back to find and correct the mistake. On the other hand, if Sally, who struggled greatly with chemistry, brought the same assignment to her teacher to prove her mastery of an objective, we used a different standard. We first checked for essential understanding that would ensure her success in future objectives. If those essentials were met, we would probably let a few minor errors slide.

We should point out a few qualifiers about this system. We are very careful to not let students move on without a solid grasp of essential objectives. Letting them do so would simply set them up for future failure. In addition, this short anecdote could sound as if we pigeonhole students early in the year and assess them only on our perceptions of the students. Under the flipped-mastery model, we interact with the students on such a regular basis, and we know them so well, that we constantly modify our expectations for each student as they mature as scientists and as learners. We recognize that our students are not programmable machines, but come to us with different backgrounds and needs. Our job as teachers is to be perpetually aware of those backgrounds and needs and to guide each student to the desired end in a way that is meaningful to each individual. Essentially, these differentiated, informal, formative assessments are different for every student, and our expectations change daily.

The mastery model makes learning the center of the classroom

Walk into a classroom in which you find the teacher standing in front of the room talking to students. What is the center of this classroom? It is the teacher. If the teacher is dynamic and can clearly communicate a subject, the students are fortunate. But even then, the focus of the classroom is still on the teacher.

"The point of school is to learn." This statement, made by a student of ours, gets to the heart of flipped mastery. Our classes have become laboratories of learning where the entire focus of the classroom is on what students have or have not learned. No longer do we present material, provide a few extra learning opportunities, give a test, and then hope for the best. Instead, students come to class with the express purpose of learning. We provide them with all the tools and materials to learn, and we support them by helping them develop a plan for how and when they will learn. The rest is up to the student.

Our class is more of a conversation than simply dissemination. Students are expected to come to class and continue the process of learning or demonstrating mastery of the objectives. When learning becomes the center of the classroom, the students must work just as hard as the teacher. This means their minds are engaged, not just passively being exposed to information.

To help transition the focus of education from the teacher to the students, we have begun to refer to our classrooms as *learning spaces*. The word "classroom" has a lot of baggage and emphasizes the teacher as the center. It conjures up images of a teacher in front of a class with chalk in hand, disseminating knowledge to the masses. In a classroom, the teacher talks and the students listen. In a classroom, the teacher "teaches" and hopes the students learn.

When we, as educators, start calling our classrooms learning spaces, it will force us to change the way we think about what happens there. When we communicate this name change to our students, they will realize that the point of school is to learn, not to be taught. And as they realize the power of learning for the sake of learning, our schools will become learning spaces.

The **mastery model** gives students instant feedback and reduces teacher paperwork

The informal formative assessments mentioned earlier eliminate the need for a teacher to collect and mark mountains of paper. In addition, the students no longer have to wait days or weeks to get the necessary feedback on a particular assignment.

Typically, students bring completed work to their teacher and have a conversation about the key elements in an objective. During this conversation, we check for understanding and misconceptions. Instead of taking the student's work home, we are "grading" the work immediately with the student present. Students identify what they do not understand, and we discuss any misconceptions and plan the student's course of action to correct them. If mastery of the objective is demonstrated, we help the students plan the steps necessary for mastering the next objective. This is a powerful time for us to clear up misunderstandings, to challenge our bright students to take the objectives a step further, and to help students see the bigger picture. Often students learn an objective in isolation and do not see how it connects to other key topics. These one-on-one or small-group discussions get students to a deeper level of comprehension and understanding.

One teacher who has adopted our model, Brett Wilie from Texas, was recently tweeting about his students' reaction to him making them prove their understanding of the content. They said, "Mr. Wilie, it was easier when we did not have to teach you. Can we go back to where we just take the test?" The students' comments about flipped mastery expose the reality that learning something deeply is a lot of work. Students under a flipped-mastery model quickly realize that the point of class is not simply to get by, but rather to thrive.

Our students take the unit assessments on classroom computers. The testing program we use grades their assessment and gives them feedback immediately. After each assessment, students notify us, and we review the exam with them. We then have a conversation about what they do and do not understand. Usually, we see a pattern of mistakes that helps us develop a proper remediation plan for the student. No longer does a student have to wait for a teacher to take tests home, grade them, pass them back, and go over the test as a class. Each student is provided the timely feedback that is essential to quickly correct misconceptions that keep them from mastering the objectives. This immediate feedback is a critical element in the flipped-mastery model because students must master the objectives before moving on to the next unit.

ISTE STANDARDS IN ACTION

Facilitator (2.6.a) and Analyst (2.7.b)

To help students think more critically about course content, work independently, and take ownership of their own learning, I use project-based learning (PBL) in my teacher preparatory course. In small groups, students have to create a new and improved school by applying what they have learned about the foundations of education to an invented school. The project is called the Design-A-School project and the essential question asks "How can we improve schools to better meet the needs of 21st century diverse learners?" For example, these future teachers learn about the issue of teacher burnout by watching a documentary and reading a few articles before coming to class. They must, then with their group, discuss and discover through additional research how their invented school might help prevent teacher burnout. Groups can choose their focus such as mental health, administration support, hiring practices, professional development opportunities, or any other ideas to alleviate teacher burnout. The end product of the Design-A-School project is the creation of a website for their new school that incorporates all of the units in the foundations of education course: being a teacher, purpose of education, school reform, history of education, philosophy of education, finance and governance of schools, and educational technology. Using PBL and flipped learning in the classroom fosters a culture of student-led learning, and the scaffolded design of creating one webpage at a time gives me the opportunity to provide feedback to groups throughout the project. Design-A-School groups present their completed website at the end of the semester as a summative assessment.

Scan the QR code to view a graphic designed in ThingLink that provides detailed information about the Design-A-School project-based learning activity used in a teacher preparatory program at Molloy

Design-A-School   University in New York.

—MADELINE CRAIG, ED.D. ASSOCIATE PROFESSOR, SCHOOL OF EDUCATION AND HUMAN SERVICES MOLLOY UNIVERSITY, ROCKVILLE CENTRE, NY

The **mastery model** provides opportunities for remediation

Not every student demonstrates mastery on the first attempt. What happens when a student does not learn the first time? In a traditional classroom, the class moves on with or without students who do not understand. The pace of the class is set by the teacher and is based on the material that is to be delivered on that particular day. Under this model, some students get further behind, their grades suffer, and they are penalized for being slower. We do not penalize our slower students. Instead, we give them ample opportunities to relearn and remediate.

Built into the immediate feedback is time for us to work with students and catch misunderstandings and misconceptions. As we circulate around our rooms, we are constantly giving students feedback on their learning progress. Typically, this looks like one of us going up to a student or a group of students and asking to see what they are working on. We then check their progress either by examining the product they are working on or through guided questions. If we see problems in their under-standing, we correct their misconceptions on the spot. This immediate feedback stops many problems from ever occurring.

Usually, there are some students in each unit who are struggling to understand some particular objectives. We identify these students and spend some time with them in small groups and hold a brief reteach/review session. According to some of the students, this attention has been some of the best learning time they have had. When students take the unit assessment, some invariably do not score satisfactorily. These students work with the teacher individually to identify the best course of remediation. What we notice is that students are not connecting all of the pieces and are failing to grasp a few key concepts. Once these misconceptions are cleared up, students are ready to move on.

The **mastery model** allows for multiple means of learning content

We recently were introduced to Universal Design for Learning (UDL), a learning theory that originated at Harvard University. The basic tenets of UDL are providing students with multiple means of representation, multiple means of expression, and multiple means of engagement (CAST, 2018).

Our primary concern is student mastery of our objectives. We realize that not all students learn best from our videos. In order to give students multiple means of representation, we provide other options for students to learn. In addition to the videos, assignments, and labs, each set of objectives references the applicable sections in the student textbook. Many students learn from our videos, others learn from textbooks, and others find information about our objectives via the internet. One size does not fit all, and we no longer require students to view the videos if they choose not to.

Allowing students choice in how to learn has empowered them. Students realize that their learning is their own responsibility. Teaching them this life lesson is more important than our science content. Students have the freedom to learn using their best learning strategies. One of the consequences of this is that students are discovering how they best learn. By giving the students the choice in how they learn something, we give them ownership of their own learning.

ISTE STANDARD IN ACTION

Designer (2.5.c)

I witnessed the impact UDL can have on student learning when I worked with our grade 7 Science teacher on her yearly ecosystem project. In this project, students are asked to design and implement an ecosystem all within a closed container. Students use an engineering design process to monitor and report on progress, as well as reflect on their design thinking. In an earlier version of the project, this teacher utilized a rather large file of Google slides as the Digital Lab Notebook, and it became large and hard to easily manage as more content was added.

We decided a Google site for each team's materials, observations, and inferences would provide a better organizational structure. She created the layout of the various tabs and organized areas where reference material could be stored, so students could have easy access to key background information as well as process diagrams. In the end, we designed a template site, where the student engineers could interact with the entire design process from asking a question, researching the larger problem, planning their project, and building a prototype.

Ecosystem Engineering Project

The key was demonstrating mastery of the learning objectives, but how that was demonstrated was up to each team. She allowed teams to add photos of their build day, reflections on their design process, as well as notes about what aspects of their prototype they wanted to evaluate. The result was a wide variety of "notebooks" (scan the QR code for an example) that were as individual as each team.

—JOHN PADULA, TECHNOLOGY INTEGRATION SPECIALIST, HOPKINTON, MA

The assignments we give provide several ways for students to demonstrate learning. In the past we required every student to complete every problem of every assignment to our satisfaction. Now, we are at the point where we do not care how a student learns an objective—we simply want them to learn it. We provide the students with appropriate videos, worksheets, and labs that we believe will help all students master our objectives. We ask the students to essentially "prove" to us that they are approaching mastery of each objective.

The **mastery model** provides multiple chances for demonstrating understanding

Another key element of UDL we have implemented is providing students multiple methods of expression. These methods should be flexible and allow for student choice. When we started the flipped-mastery model, we insisted students get at least 75% on every unit assessment.

When we reflected on how we were assessing students, we realized one size doesn't fit all. We discussed with our students that they could demonstrate understanding of the objectives in multiple ways. We now allow students multiple ways of proving their mastery of the objectives, including:

- Summative unit exams

- Verbal discussions

- Detailed PowerPoint presentations

- Short videos

- Demonstration of understanding written in prose

- Other methods developed by the students

Recently, Jonathan had a student who asked if he could just discuss what he had learned instead of writing out a detailed paragraph. Although there is certainly value in writing, his explanation was thorough and complete. He understood what was being taught, but explaining it orally was easier for him and also played into his verbal skills.

Jonathan had another student who texted him and asked if he could make a video game for his assessment. Jonathan approved his alternative assessment proposal without any idea of what the product would look like. This student, Nic, set the new bar for innovative assessments. Nic walked into class a few days after the text with his video game console, plugged it into the class projector, and proceeded to astound us as he demonstrated the game and his understanding of the learning objectives. Jonathan was so amazed that he immediately texted Aaron. He was so excited that the text was unintelligible and Aaron had to go to Jonathan's classroom just to interpret the message. When Aaron arrived, he was just as dumbfounded as Jonathan at the way Nic creatively demonstrated his understanding. Aaron immediately pulled out his video camera to document this example. Shortly after, Jonathan had students clamoring to play the game, and some even asked if playing and "beating" the game levels (learning objectives) could be their assessment. This student later enrolled in our Senior Seminar course where he developed more of these game-based assessments. He left these as a legacy for future students at our high school.

Aaron had a student who struggled with the computer-based tests. This student chose to hand write, in prose form, everything he knew about each objective. He could clearly communicate his understanding and always provided mathematical examples that differed from any examples given in the videos or the assignments. He clearly understood the concepts, but simply struggled to demonstrate his knowledge on the teacher-generated exam.

All of these students are able to clearly prove their mastery of the objectives, but would not have been able to do so had we not married the UDL principles to the flipped-mastery model.

The **mastery model** changes the role of the teacher

The flipped-mastery model changes the role of the teacher. Instead of standing in front of the room spewing information and being the center of attention, we spend our time doing what is most important: helping students, leading small groups, and working with individuals who are struggling. We find ourselves walking around the room visiting with students about key learning objectives. The best analogy we can come up with is the role of a supportive coach. We are there to encourage our students along the road of learning. They need a coach who can come alongside them and guide them in the discovery of knowledge. We have more opportunities to encourage students and tell them what they are doing right, as well as to clear up their misconceptions.

This changes the dynamics of class. Class time is a learning experience for the student, not a download and upload of knowledge. When we first started out, Jonathan in particular had a hard time giving up the direct instruction. He was a pretty good lecturer. But in time, as he saw all of his students genuinely learning, he readily gave up whole-class direct instruction.

The **mastery model** teaches students the value of learning instead of "playing" school

How often have you had students in your classroom who are good at "playing" school? They come to class more interested in getting a grade than in learning. They tend to be the first ones to ask for extra credit and tend to want rote-memory questions on exams rather than deeper, more insightful ones. Sadly, our educational system has failed these students by perpetuating an environment in which success is measured by the ability to recall information. Though they may be able to regurgitate that information for an exam, they haven't truly learned.

When these students enter our flipped-mastery classroom, they typically get frustrated. They have spent many years learning to play the game of school and have not developed the ability to really learn. Flipped mastery forces them to learn instead of memorize. We have seen tremendous growth in these students. They enter our course frustrated and leave as learners.

The **mastery model** is easily reproducible, scalable, and customizable

At a recent conference we received some interesting positive feedback from one of our participants. He said that flipped mastery is easily scalable. What we are doing can be reproduced and customized simply in a variety of educational settings. Practicing teachers see flipped mastery as a tool they can easily implement.

In the early 2000s, Dwight Jones, the former commissioner of education for the state of Colorado, came to visit our district. Jonathan happened to be in our central office and was brought into the conversation about the flipped-mastery model. Jones was very interested in the model and wanted to know more. We took him down to our classroom, and he had a chance to talk with a student. Afterward, Jones made an interesting comment: "And all of this happened in Woodland Park!" He caught himself, and then said he meant that it did not come out of one of the larger, richer, "premier" school districts in our state. The point is: if it can be done in our little town with minimal resources, it can be done anywhere.

To continue that point, we started this in a chemistry class—a class with dangerous chemicals and significant safety concerns! As we've shared the flipped-mastery model around the country, most people think we were crazy to develop it in a chemistry class. But we saw the potential of the model, we happen to be chemistry teachers, and we thought it was best for kids. And we were right! So, if flipped mastery can be successfully implemented in a small town, with no resources, in a dangerous chemistry class, it can be implemented anywhere.

The **mastery model** increases face-to-face time with the teacher

As we began to use the flipped-mastery model, some parents expressed concern that the amount of student–teacher interaction would decrease. One parent said it well: "I have to admit I was skeptical about the [videos] at first. I had a fear that they would reduce the amount of direct contact with the students and questions about the lectures would go unanswered. I am happy to say I was very wrong. You have come up with a way to increase the amount of teaching time for your class, and I feel my son is doing very well with it." Flipped mastery leads to much more student–teacher interaction.

 Simply by making videos for my lectures, I was able to save 50 days of instruction. This extra time freed me up to start doing more hands-on activities and experiments with the students. I finally had time to properly have students apply the content from their notes. This has deepened their understanding of the content."

—Bob Furlong, High School Biology Teacher, Otsego High School, Otsego, MI

The **mastery model** ensures that all students are involved

In a flipped-mastery class, all students are in charge of their own learning. Years ago Jonathan was a trainer in the field of brain-based research and its implications in education. He often used this sentence to summarize the research: "The brain of someone who is working is growing." When you walk into a typical classroom, whose brain is usually working? In many classrooms, you see the teacher standing in front of students, probably with a PowerPoint lesson, maybe even on an interactive whiteboard, talking to the students. Sadly, it is the teacher's brain that is working the hardest and thus growing, while the students' brains are much less active as they sit passively.

A flipped-mastery classroom looks significantly different. Students are engaged in a variety of activities. Some are taking assessments, some are watching a video on a portable device, some are involved in a discussion with their teacher, some are engaged in hands-on activities, and some are working in small learning groups. Whose brain is now working? Clearly, it is the brains of the students.

The **mastery model** makes hands-on activities more personal

Hands-on activities help students learn in a way other than direct instruction. This is particularly true in the subject of science. Students cannot just learn about science; they have to *do* science to learn. As students conduct experiments, they are experiencing science and constructing knowledge of scientific concepts. When done well, these hands-on activities help students question, process, and analyze what they have done.

Before flipped mastery, we would conduct these hands-on activities in a large group. The whole class would receive instructions on the experiment, and all of the students would conduct the activity simultaneously. From an organizational perspective, this is very efficient, but it is not necessarily what is best for kids. Because the flipped-mastery model is asynchronous, students conduct the experiments when they are ready to do so. The time varies from student to student. We typically work with groups of four to five students conducting an experiment. Before the experiment, we have a discussion with the group that covers the purpose of the activity and the pertinent safety concerns. Because we're discussing this in a small group, we can look the kids in the eye and see if they understand both what they will be doing and how to do it safely. Students are more engaged in these hands-on activities when they are in more intimate groups. We feel that our students are safer as a result of receiving individualized safety instructions.

The **mastery model** makes teacher-led demonstrations more engaging

Similar to labs, a key component in most science courses is teacher-led demonstrations. In our chemistry course we boil water by adding ice, we burn paper with steam, and we have students light us on fire. In the past, we conducted these demonstrations as part of our lecture in front of the whole class. Under the flipped model, we still did these as whole-class demonstrations. When we demonstrated a concept to a class of 30, only a few students in the "good seats" could see what was happening, and only a few could participate because of time constraints. In addition, only a few students (usually the bright kids who already had all the answers) participated in the discussion.

Now that our classes are asynchronous, we conduct these demonstrations when students are ready for them. This means we conduct the demonstration multiple times for a given class over the course of a few weeks in front of smaller groups of students. In smaller groups, all students can see what is happening; all of them are huddled around the interesting demonstration. In the case where our students light us on fire, it used to be that one or two students would light us on fire for any given class. Now we have all the students light us on fire. Thus, when their parents ask them what they did in school today, they can proudly say: "I lit my teacher on fire."

We find that these more personal demonstrations increase understanding. Conducting demonstrations under the flipped-mastery model allows all kids to participate in the discussion instead of waiting for the bright kid to chime in with the "answer." Dividing up students into smaller demonstration groups is one of the key changes that make the flipped-mastery model so successful. Students receive a more personalized education on a daily basis.

> Flipped learning has changed my teaching by allowing students to work at their own pace. Students are able to work ahead to challenge themselves and get extra support when needed. With the many absences throughout the pandemic, flipped learning was my saving grace to be able to help students that were gone for large blocks of time and to help students with online learning!"
>
> —Julie Buerman, Chemistry Teacher, Cedar Rapids Kennedy High School, Cedar Rapids, IA

The mastery model helps teachers help kids

As we visit with teachers, we find them frustrated with students who are not learning. Teachers want to do what is best for their students. Flipped mastery got us back to the reason we entered the teaching profession: to help kids. Flipped mastery is all about the students.

We began this on a shoestring budget and were able to transform our classes in a deep and fundamental way. The most remarkable aspect of our journey is realizing that we are not doing anything new! For millennia, students have been expected to come to class prepared to discuss and interact with knowledge they have already been exposed to. Unfortunately, somewhere in human history the lecture wedged its way into our instructional toolbox, and schools have been digging their way out from under its oppression ever since. We have simply adapted several very good learning principles and married them by leveraging modern technology to change the face of teaching. Mastery learning, Universal Design for Learning, project-based learning, objective/standards-based grading, and educational technology were all tapped to help create the flipped-mastery model of teaching.

CHAPTER 7

how to implement
the flipped-mastery model

So, now you are convinced. You want to implement some form of a flipped-mastery classroom.
But you have questions and concerns. There are
so many logistical details you need to work out.
What about X? What about Y? What will this even
look like in your circumstances? Although there
are similarities among teachers who have flipped
their classes, clearly there is no such thing as *the*
flipped class, so where do you start? We have been
using the flipped-mastery model since 2008, and
we have made a lot of mistakes—mistakes you do
not have to make. As we've said before, we want
you to learn from our mistakes and improve on the
model. Since the publication of the first edition of

this book thousands of teachers around the world have adopted the flipped-mastery model, and we have learned so much from those who have shared their journeys and experiences. In the following sections, we'll try to condense all we've learned into a few short tips to get you started. For a deeper dive, consult Jonathan's book *The Mastery Learning Handbook: A Competency-Based Approach to Student Achievement* (2022), which tackles the nitty-gritty details about how to implement mastery learning in your classroom from the beginning.

What to Do on the First Day

Introductory Video

When we started the flipped-mastery model, we thought it would be best to ease our students into the model. We started out by getting all students to watch the same video on the same night. We essentially implemented a regular flipped model and then transitioned into a flipped-mastery model. As it turns out, that was a mistake.

Testimonial Video

In the first year of implementation, we had hoped that keeping the students together for the first unit would allow time for students to figure out any technical hurdles and for us to ease them into this model, which was so different from anything else they had encountered. We completely underestimated our students. They adapted quickly, and when we switched them from flipped to flipped-mastery, we caused unnecessary confusion. As any seasoned teacher knows, the first few weeks of school are essential for establishing policies and routines. Training the students in one model and switching the procedures after three weeks is not good classroom management practice.

Now, we start the year by immediately introducing the students to the flipped-mastery model. We answer questions and spend a fair amount of time discussing how important it is for the students to take responsibility for their learning. Students watch short videos we made explaining the model. Jonathan now uses two videos to start out the year. In the first one he explains the reason he uses mastery learning, and in the second one he uses testimonials from past students that give advice to his current group. (Scan the QR codes to see examples of the videos.) We found that when students hear from their peers they are much more likely to take the advice than they would be if they heard the same from us teachers.

Flipped mastery has become a part of the culture of our science department. Our principal told us it generally takes about three years for something to become culture in a school. The first year is the hardest, the second year all the bugs get worked out, and the third year it becomes part of the school culture. This pattern is exactly what we experienced as we implemented the flipped-mastery model. By our third year, flipped mastery had become culture, and the model was running smoothly.

Find Out Which Students Are Ready for Self-Direction

Flipped Learning Readiness

Mastery learning requires students to be more self-directed, and not all students are initially ready for that level of freedom and choice. To that end, it is helpful to know which students will need additional support for self-direction. Hatice Yildiz Durak of Bartin University, Turkey (Durak, 2018) created a survey that determines which students are ready for self-directed learning. The survey includes items related to students' control over their learning, self-sufficiency with technology, in-class communication, motivation for learning, and readiness to do preliminary work for class. Giving this kind of survey at the beginning of the year helps teachers focus in on those students who will need more direction on their semi-self-paced lessons.

We applied her research to significantly alter her initial study questions to meet the needs of our students. To learn more about her work in this space and how to apply it to your own classroom, scan the QR code.

Inform Parents About the Model

Explanatory Video for Parents

We inform parents by sending a letter home explaining the model. Parents need to be educated about the model because it is something new. In Jonathan's current class he sends a video home explaining the model to parents (scan the QR code to see an example). Explaining it this way has enhanced the teacher–parent communication. By and large, it takes constant communication with parents to help them understand both what we are doing and why we are doing it. But when we communicate to parents the advantages of the flipped-mastery model, they see how their children will benefit, and parents are generally in favor.

Early in implementation, there was some pushback from parents, but as time has gone on, they have come to accept flipped mastery as the way we do business.

Teach Students How to Watch and Interact with the Videos

An essential first step is to teach your students how to watch the videos. This is similar to teaching students to read and use a textbook. Watching an instructional video is not like watching a movie or TV show for entertainment. These educational videos need to be watched with the same focus you would read a nonfiction book as opposed to the latest thriller. We encourage students to eliminate distractions: They shouldn't try to watch the video with Facebook open and AirPods in their ears while simultaneously texting and making dinner. To train students, we take some time the first few days of school to watch some videos together. We make liberal use of the Pause button. We pause the video for the students and highlight key points. At one point we give control of the Pause and Rewind features to one student. Invariably, the student in control of the Pause and Rewind buttons processes the information at a different pace than most of the class. All students want to control the video, which of course, is the point. After watching one of these videos as a class, we discuss with them how much better it would be if all of them had control of their own Pause buttons. Of course, they will have control for the rest of the year, but demonstrating this helps them see the value of the videos and, more importantly, their control over their own learning.

During this training period, we also teach them effective note-taking skills. There are many great ways to take notes, but we are fans of the Cornell note-taking system. We give them a template for Cornell notes and have them use this system not only to write down key points, but also to ask questions and summarize what they have learned.

 ## ISTE STANDARD IN ACTION

Analyst (2.7.a)

In our grade 8 literature circles, we attempted to have students "see themselves" in action. Rather than rely on just observation feedback from a classroom teacher, the ELA teacher and I constructed literature circle sessions that allowed students to be filmed in action. Students signed up for various roles within the group and were given advanced notice that their literature circle sessions would be filmed. We also made it clear that the videos would serve in part as their demonstration of competency.

When filming was over, we wanted students to learn, reflect, and grow from their first week of literature circle work. Rather than set up a high-stakes, all-or-nothing atmosphere, the book discussions were split across two weeks and students were tasked with reviewing their "performance" and completing a self-reflection and assessment, which they submitted at the end of week 1. The process was repeated for the second half of their book; students changed roles, and another round of filming was done. Following week 2, students were asked to reflect on their latest performance and compare it to week 1's.

What we observed was quite striking. In week 2, students were much more aware of their roles within the literature circle. Time was better spent—to the point that several groups actually asked if they could have more time in their session! Overall, the quality of the discussions and the interaction among group members was much higher. We felt it was a win for everyone!

—JOHN PADULA, TECHNOLOGY INTEGRATION SPECIALIST, HOPKINTON, MA

Require Students to Ask Interesting Questions

When we check whether or not students have watched a video, one requirement is that they ask us interesting questions. This works especially well in our freshman Earth and Space Science course. Each question must be related to the video, and the student asking it should not already know the answer. These interactions with the students are some of the richest times we experience in our classrooms. Students ask questions either individually or in small groups. Every student must ask at least one question per video. Often during these question-and-answer times, students ask us questions for which we don't know the answer, and we work together with the students on researching the answer. The questions students ask often reveal their misconceptions and inform us of what we have not taught clearly. We then have time to clarify their misunderstandings, and we make notes of corrections to make in our videos in the future to prevent further misconceptions. These interactions are truly one of the magical moments we experience every day with our students.

Every student must ask at least one question about each video. This is especially valuable for students who do not generally interact with their teachers. In the "sit and get" model, a minority of the students ask the majority of the questions. The students asking questions are typically more outgoing and confident. The quiet, introspective students often have the same questions, but rarely voice those in the traditional model. In the flipped-mastery model all students must ask questions. We have received more and better questions in our courses than we ever did in a traditional model, and the discussions have been richer. We have found that students are curious, and in this nonthreatening format, all students can demonstrate their curiosity and learn in an individualized way.

ISTE STANDARD IN ACTION

Analyst (2.7.b)

In my flipped and fully online courses, I use Edpuzzle for interactive video watching by uploading the videos I create into Edpuzzle and adding assessments throughout the video. When my students view the video, it pauses to have students answer either a multiple-choice question, a short answer, or a short write-in response. I also like adding short comments to bring to the students' attention key phrases or important definitions. Edpuzzle makes video watching an interactive experience rather than a passive one and allows me to assess student learning. I can easily integrate Edpuzzle into our learning management system, Canvas, which simplifies grading since it is built into my existing gradebook. As the final question in the Edpuzzle, I ask my students "What one final question do you have?" and then I answer these questions in our face-to-face class in an effort to bridge our online and in-person classes.

—MADELINE CRAIG, ED.D. ASSOCIATE PROFESSOR, SCHOOL OF EDUCATION AND HUMAN SERVICES MOLLOY UNIVERSITY, ROCKVILLE CENTRE, NY

Another thing we have noticed during the question-and-answer times is how our quiet students come out of their shells. Sadly, some of our students rarely have adults listen to them. Their parents are too busy, and their teachers are talking to them. The only people who will listen to them are their peers. These conversational times have opened up a chance to get to know our students on a more personal level, which has paid dividends in helping troubled teens through difficult times.

Set Up Your Classroom for Flipped Mastery

We used to set up our rooms in a traditional format. The center of the room was the teacher, which usually meant all desks faced the chalkboard. As we got more technological, all desks faced the screen, which was hooked up to a projector. As we began implementing our flipped-mastery model, we realized that we even needed to rethink the geography of our rooms. Now our flipped-mastery classroom is designed around learning (picture a kindergarten class). Instead of the focus of the room being toward the front, it is now focused toward the middle. This shift changes the psychology of the students. They see learning as the center of the room instead of the teacher. We both have projectors in our rooms, but they are rarely turned on. The focus of the room is the learning, not the teacher presentation.

We also each have an interactive whiteboard (IWB) mounted on the side of the room instead of at the front. Students now routinely use the IWBs as interactive tools for learning, but when we first received them, one student asked hesitantly if she could touch the board. She obviously had seen one in use, but only as a tool for the teacher. In our classrooms, students use the IWBs to manipulate online science simulations, collaborate on projects, and simply explore new ways of learning and understanding. For example, in our Earth and Space Science class, we use a program that turns any computer into a virtual telescope aimed at the night sky. Students can change the date and the location and observe constellations in different hemispheres or track planetary movements. The IWB is a hub of activity as students flock to the board to learn about the stars and more.

> Students have more control over mastery of content and subject matter. They can rework assignments and view materials as many times as needed until they feel prepared to move on to meet new challenges. It puts students in charge of their learning."
>
> —Beth Hammett, Associate Professor of English, College of the Mainland, Texas City, TX

We teach science, and science, if done right, requires many hands-on activities. Most of these are experiments. We are often asked how we set up the experiments for a system where students could be conducting different experiments at the same time. We think the best analogy is that of an elementary classroom where there are centers around the room. One center is for reading, one for writing, one for working on a computer, and so on. Our classrooms are set up in a similar fashion. We have one station for an experiment on reaction types, another set up for single replacement reactions, and another set up as an empirical formula lab. We use less equipment than before because only a few students do an experiment at a time, and safety is improved because we spend time talking to smaller groups about key safety procedures before each experiment. From a financial perspective, a flipped-mastery classroom is cheaper because only a fraction of the necessary equipment and materials are required. You'll please your administration when you begin to operate on 20% of your former budget.

Allow Students to Manage Their Time and Workload

Jonathan's daughter was a student in his flipped-mastery class for two years. As one December approached, she became concerned about the stress of the end of a semester and her grade in her classes. Finals were in two weeks; she had a big dance recital and a church play; and all of her class assignments were due. One thing she really liked about the flipped-mastery model was that it allowed her to manage her own time. She used a good portion of her Thanksgiving break to get ahead in her dad's class. She realized her life was about to get really busy, so she chose to work ahead. She realized she could take her final once she mastered all of the semester objectives. So, she planned her time so the rest of her upcoming schedule was not quite as crazy. She took and passed her final exam early and was able to focus on her other classes. She even used her dad's class time as an opportunity to prepare for her other class finals.

She is not alone. One thing we notice about our students is they learn to manage their own time. They know which objectives need to be mastered by a particular time. They can pace their schedules and learn to make good choices about priorities and time management.

Jonathan's daughter was a conscientious student who wanted to excel. You are probably asking, "What about students who don't take as much initiative?" We find our flipped-mastery classes to be great growing experiences for our students. Those who come in with few time-management skills learn to manage their time. We give students freedom to make both good and bad choices. As the year progresses, students begin to make better and better choices. We see this with our struggling student population as well as our honors students. Although the flipped-mastery model is not the magic bullet for developing all students' time management skills, it certainly has led to growth for most of our students.

Encourage Kids to Help Kids

We describe our classes as *hubs of learning*. The focus of the classroom is no longer on the teacher, but rather on the learning. Subsequently, students realize that learning is the goal and turn to each other for help. They automatically organize themselves into learning groups. It is very common for us to walk by a group, ask about what they're learning, and see students helping others.

We also place students into strategic groups. We find students who are struggling with the same content and assemble a spontaneous group. This dynamic keeps the class from becoming a place in which 30 students are conducting independent study. The small groups maintain the classroom dynamic by encouraging interaction, collaboration, and exploration.

All of this excites us. Our students realize they're better when they work as a team rather than when they work alone. This gets at the heart of digital age learning: students working together to accomplish the same goals. We realize they will soon enter the world of work, and people rarely work in isolation. The students will become part of teams solving problems, and the flipped-mastery model is set up to encourage this kind of interaction.

Build an Appropriate Assessment System

Certainly, one of the biggest challenges in our model is building an appropriate assessment system that objectively measures student understanding in a way that is meaningful for the students and the teacher. How do I know if my students have mastered the course objectives? What do I do when students don't get it? These questions invariably present a challenge to those interested in adopting the flipped-mastery model. But fear not: We have learned the hard way, so you don't have to.

ISTE STANDARD IN ACTION

Analyst (2.7.a)

Providing student choice is a key component to increasing student engagement whether in a flipped classroom or a classroom operating under other models. Technology provides us with the ability to offer students this choice without adding extra work on teachers. For example, using a This or That–style choice board allows students to work through a playlist that moves them through the learning process with some aspect of choice. The flipped model is one of several that can be offered in this type of choice board. During the Explore and Learn portions of the choice board, students might have the option to watch a video or to read a text. As they move into the Create category, students can then create their own videos that help demonstrate their learning or do some type of digital sketchnotes. For their own self-created videos, students can use tools like Flip, Screencastify, WeVideo, or a video tool embedded in a school's learning management system (Canvas Studio for instance). Finally, students can reflect in a variety of ways on the learning experience through the use of LMS discussion boards, Google Forms, or even a Padlet activity. Providing these choices allows students more agency in their learning, but it also allows for students to use a method that meets their individual learning needs.

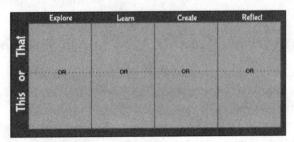

—TIFFANY REXHAUSEN, INNOVATION SPECIALIST, LAKOTA LOCAL SCHOOLS/LIBERTY JUNIOR SCHOOL, LIBERTY TOWNSHIP, OH

The logistics of managing multiple versions of one assessment is possibly what derailed the mastery movement in the 1980s. Creating multiple versions of quality assessments, managing the paper, and keeping track of test security is just too overwhelming for one teacher with 30 students in a room. We believe that leveraging modern technology to provide valuable feedback to our students and to aid us in implementing the flipped-mastery model is what makes mastery possible.

Formative Assessments

Both of us have taught chemistry for many years, and over that time we've developed enough background in our subject to quickly tell whether a student understands key points. As we move around the room and interact with students, we spot-check their understanding. While students are in the process of learning, we discover and correct misconceptions. We recognize that as students develop concepts, they require different levels of support depending on their individual cognitive development as well as the cognitive load of a particular objective. At times, we provide a student with very structured assistance, but in other situations, we allow students to struggle. We realize that learning is not a matter of spoon-feeding the content to the students. It is appropriate for the teacher to allow a student to wrestle with a difficult concept so that the student learns it deeply. So, some students we leave alone, because we know their learning will be much deeper than if we hold their hand throughout, and we proceed to provide support to students who need it.

The burden of proof in the formative process is placed on the student. We provide students with learning objectives and the resources necessary to meet those objectives, but the students are required to provide evidence to the teacher that the objective is being learned. For students who can't prove that they are making progress toward the objective, we quickly assess their understanding and create a customized remediation plan on the spot so students can go back and learn what they have not yet mastered. The types of remediation and reteaching vary from student to student. We may ask the student to rewatch a specific video or, in some cases, to watch it for the first time. We give them textbook resources to consult and web pages to visit, or we may simply sit down with them and work through the concepts they don't understand. We used to refer to the formative assessment process as "checking the oil," but in a conversation with Ewan McIntosh, he corrected us and equated formative assessment to a GPS. When a driver using a GPS begins to go astray, the GPS "recalculates" the route to help the driver get back on track. The driver can continue to ignore the GPS, but it will continue to recalculate a route to the desired destination. Eventually, the driver will listen to the ever-persistent GPS and get back on track—or, as McIntosh puts it, drive into a lake. In the classroom, the teacher can be the voice of the GPS, redirecting students when they go astray in their understanding. Students can accept the advice and redirection of the teacher, or they can drive themselves into the cognitive lake of misconception. It is the responsibility of the teacher to constantly evaluate each student's path and provide immediate feedback that will keep the student traveling safely through the highways of learning. Ultimately, the key questions are always, "Did you learn it? And if you did, can you provide evidence that you have?" However, part of good teaching is knowing where the student is along the journey, not just checking to see if they arrived safely.

Asking the Right Formative Assessment Questions

As we interact with our students, we are constantly having a dialogue with them. We're making sure they understand the learning objectives. We're prodding them and pushing them to learn as deeply as they can. A key component of this is our questioning strategy. Some time ago we sat down with the dean of the school of education at a private university. She was most curious about this aspect of the flipped-mastery process and pointed out that we were veteran teachers who intuitively knew which questions to ask. How, she wondered, would we would train new teachers in our methodology?

> In flipped learning, I observed that the assigned pre-class learning duties reduced students' cognitive load during the chemistry sessions. The student-centered in-class activities helped my students to overcome their misconceptions in some difficult topics, such as structural isomerism, IUPAC nomenclature, chemical bonding, and so on. Also, the flipped-classroom framework allows me to incorporate other pedagogies based on the need to enhance my students' conceptual understanding."
>
> —S. Athavan Alias Anand, Senior Researcher, Department of Chemistry, Prayoga Institute of Education Research, Bengaluru, Karnataka, India

This is a tricky question to answer, because intuition is not easily transferable. We deliberately take time early each school year to discover and understand how each student thinks and learns. We don't do this with any formal battery of assessments; we simply talk to our students and get to know them. Our method is highly subjective, but it works. So, our advice to other teachers interested in adopting the flipped-mastery model is to talk to your students, get to know them as the amazing people they are, learn how they think, and help them learn how to learn.

The teacher must ask the right question for each individual student. Because we know our students well, and because we know to what extent they understand each learning objective, we vary our questions based on student understanding. Each student is at a different level of comprehension, and our main goal is growth.

One advantage of flipped mastery is that the teacher gets a lot of practice asking questions. Instead of asking the question one time during a lecture, you get to ask students as you interact with each of them. Practicing the flipped-mastery model will help prospective teachers by giving them ample opportunities to tailor specific questions to students and meet their individual learning needs.

Summative Assessments

Our formative assessments are essential in checking student understanding, and they are fundamental in the formation of student content knowledge. However, we believe that students also need high-stakes assessments in which they demonstrate their mastery of learning objectives. Thus, we have developed summative assessments for which students must demonstrate a minimum level of proficiency.

Various models of assessment exist for the educator. Exams can be scored out of total points, objectives can be assessed individually on a 0–4 scale, or a test can represent a straight percentage. We live in an A–F world where percentages determine a student's letter grade. Although we don't entirely believe in assessing students using a percentage, we nonetheless have to operate under a less-than-ideal framework. In order to function in the A–F environment that parents, students, and administrators are comfortable with, we've decided that students need to score a minimum of 75% on every summative assessment in order to prove mastery. This number is not arbitrary. We look at the essential learning objectives and create the test such that if a student has mastered the key objectives, they will score a 75%. The other 25% of the assessment can be earned by mastering the "nice to know" objectives that are also a part of our curriculum, but may not be essential for success in subsequent lessons. If a student does not score 75% or higher, then they must retake the assessment. If a student struggles with a specific topic, we provide remediation to him or her, giving the support the student needs to master each summative assessment. We also allow a student to retake an assessment if a 75% is attained but the student desires a higher score. We leave this up to students, because we are also trying to teach them to take responsibility for their own learning.

We have a number of laboratory assessments students must complete. In these assessments, students are given a problem to solve. They then use available equipment, chemicals, and materials to work out the solution to the problem. These authentic assessments are also a key part of our program. Students also need to score a minimum of 75% to move on with these. One of the benefits of the flipped-mastery model for the students is that they are not allowed to turn in junk. If they submit unacceptable reports, we simply hand them back and make them fix their work. Students who are just trying to "get by" quickly discover that they're better off turning in quality work the first time instead of poor work they will have to redo.

Also note that although the process just described is the one we employ, it is not the only way to use summative assessment in a flipped-mastery setting. Many teachers and schools who have flipped administer summative assessments in a more traditional manner. The test is given to all students on a particular day, and whatever score is attained is permanent. There is no single way to flip, no single way to assess, and no single way to give students feedback. As always, do what is best for your students and operate within the parameters of your particular educational setting.

Test Integrity

When we first started the flipped-mastery program, we used paper tests. Granted, we had multiple versions, but students took the exams at different times, often in less supervised environments. Unfortunately, some of our students made poor choices and found ways to cheat on the exams. Some took pictures of the test with cell phones and shared those with their friends. Quickly, some of our exams got out into the wild among the student population.

Implementing computer testing helped with security, but even then, we found students who would copy and paste whole exams, send the copy to their home account, and distribute it to their friends. Needless to say, we were frustrated and discouraged. Because of the lack of computers in our classroom, we sometimes sent students to the school library to take exams. Sadly, we discovered students taking their exams in a group, or with notes or other unallowable materials.

Since the writing of the first edition of this book, students have gotten much more tech-savvy. At Jonathan's current school, students are all given a device and many of them have learned how to game the system. His current system involves a monitoring program (GoGuardian) and he has set the controls such that students can access the school's learning management system (D2L Brightspace) only. If you want even more security, there are a variety of lock-down browser programs and even ones that make a student download a test offline, which then turns off all access to the internet.

We are not naive. We realize that some students will always try to get around the rules and will make poor choices. Our role as good teachers is to limit the opportunity for students to cheat. With a few subtle adjustments, our present solution has solved most of our security issues. We now allow exams to happen only in class. We have set up several computers (six or seven) in our rooms. Each test is password protected, and we are the only ones who know the password. When a student is ready for an exam, the student logs on to their own account, and then the teacher types in the password. This gives us a chance to chat with each student before the exam and check to see that they have allowable references (for example, a periodic table and calculator). Usually, we give them an encouraging comment. Though this is not a perfect system, most of the integrity issues have been solved.

Those who want to take the integrity issues one step further can do what Aaron began in 2011: administer open-internet tests. He began this experiment to answer two questions:

- What questions are so easy to find answers to on the internet that they do not need to be taught in class?

- Given that so much information is at the fingertips of our students, how will the exams need to be written differently in order to effectively evaluate what the students know and can do with a certain subject?

Asking these two questions transformed his tests from primarily data-recall and mathematical computation to problem-solving, data analysis, and mathematical understanding. In addition, test integrity is less of an issue, because the answers cannot be easily shared as a result of the open-ended nature of the questions.

Logistics of Summative Assessments

When mastery learning was first being encouraged, the logistics of assessment may have been one of the main challenges that derailed widespread adoption. How does a teacher manage so many versions of a test? If we keep giving students the same exam over and over, eventually they memorize the test, but still don't understand the content. When we began the flipped-mastery model, we simply wrote a few pen-and-paper versions of each exam. Unfortunately, students did just what we feared: They memorized the exams. Although they passed the test, they had not truly learned.

Next, we turned to computer-generated exams to help us with the logistics of having to grade so many exams that were being taken at different times. At the time, our school had adopted a free, open-source course management program called Moodle, which showed great promise because it immediately graded the exams and took a great burden off of us. However, we still had the problem of too few versions of the exam that were too similar.

> By flipping learning in my classroom, I gave myself valuable time with students on an individual basis in two ways. First, they could watch the video tutorials on their own time, at their own speed, and review lessons anytime—almost like having a private tutor sitting next to them as they paused the video, tried a problem on their own, and then played the video to check their understanding. Second, I was able to 'make rounds' to each student as they worked practice problems in class to gauge understanding. Another benefit of flipped learning is that it gave me time to bring back fun, engaging games and activities to practice concepts and take learning deeper. Finally, since I flipped my classroom back in 2013, distance and hybrid learning during the pandemic were an easy transition for me and my students."
>
> —Missy Northington, Middle School Math Teacher, Saint Mary's Hall, San Antonio, TX

Our next innovation came after Jonathan read about how to use Moodle to create a unique version of each test for every student and a different version for each attempt a student makes. With this method, we created multiple questions that assessed each objective, then we had Moodle randomly choose one or more questions from each objective when we built our tests. Doing so created tens of thousands of versions of each test, solving the logistical problem of multiple versions. This truly made mastery manageable.

Be warned, though: This represents a huge amount of work. Instead of writing one or two questions for each objective, it means writing 10 to 20, which is a huge commitment. We are also continuing to refine this process and add more questions, change the way questions are worded, and make sure the essential objectives are accurately and adequately assessed. We see this as a multiple-year project that ultimately is never done.

If you are looking for course-management software in addition to Moodle, there are many other great programs out there (as discussed in Chapter 5), including Blackboard, Schoology Learning, Canvas, and D2L Brightspace. There are also dedicated assessment suites like Formative (formative.com), Quia (quia.com), and Edulastic (edulastic.com).

Working within the A–F Grading Culture

We imagine many of you work in an environment similar to ours. In our school, students still receive credit for a course completed. As teachers, we still must give all students a grade: A for excellent, B for above average, C for average, D for below average, and F for failing. We had to figure out a way to make a mastery system work in this context. At first this was a real struggle. We see our class in more of an objective-based or standards-based grading framework, but our school is not set up to operate under such a model. In addition to working a mastery model within the confines of an A–F system, we also are required to input our grades into the online grade book that our district has adopted. This grade book is visible to parents, who are accustomed to seeing all grades listed as percentages or points and calculated as a letter grade. To address these challenges, we have gone through several iterations and much reworking of our grading system.

For what it's worth, we have come up with a hybrid system that is part objective-based grading and part traditional A–F grading that may or may not work in your setting. In our system, we make summative assessments worth 50% of a student's grade. Students must score at least 75% on each summative assessment before a grade can be entered into the grade book. The other

50% of the grade is for timely progression toward mastery of individual formative assessments.

A flipped class is ideally suited to a standards-based grading (SBG) system. Many who flip do not use SBG, and many who do not use SBG do not flip; however, the two work well together. The Adams-50 school system in Westminster, Colorado, has adopted a district-wide standards-based grading system. In any given class, students can be at different grade levels, and any given student can be at different grade levels in each of his or her classes. The district instructional coaches recently discovered how well their grading system works with asynchronous video instruction, and many of their teachers are now creating videos to meet the instructional needs of their students.

Every grading environment in schools across the world is different, and we all have to operate within the parameters in which we teach. Introducing a flipped class is often a radical enough change that some may be hesitant to alter an existing grading system. This component of a flipped-mastery class will vary as much from school to school as the distribution of videos does.

flipped learning in action

With the explosion of flipped learning over the past decade, in part due to the success of the first edition of this book, teachers around the globe are using flipped learning as their primary teaching strategy. We did a quick tally of schools we have either worked with or who have contacted us, and we estimated that we have had direct contact from at least forty-seven countries. And we or people we have worked with have visited almost every corner of the globe.

Whenever we visit a school, it is rare that there isn't at least one teacher flipping their class. At this point, almost all teachers have at least heard of flipped learning and know of a colleague who has at least tried elements of it. To illustrate the impact of flipped learning on the world, this chapter presents two case studies: a single teacher who flipped his classroom and an entire school that changed its identity through flipping.

One Teacher's Journey: Matthew Moore, Warrensburg, IL

After teaching high school math in Illinois for ten years, Matthew Moore felt like he had figured out the teaching gig. He knew what to expect. He knew what things students would struggle with. He had figured out classroom management and felt like he was on the top of his game. He was the building union representative, and he had a realistic view of the key issues in education both in his classes and in his school.

A career teacher, Matthew described his teaching as extremely traditional. He taught students at all levels in his school, from the inclusion math classes up to AP Calculus. He said, "Though I taught all levels of students, I taught them all the same way: lecture, assign, record the grades." After each day's lecture, students had about ten minutes to work on the assigned problems and then they had to finish the rest at home.

Even with ten years of experience and a feeling that he had become a master teacher, Matthew still had nagging problems that he couldn't solve. One of his biggest frustrations was what to do when kids missed class. Because the content delivery happened in the class, missing one lesson really hurt his students—but it also impacted Matthew. He would spend an inordinate amount of time meeting with students who missed class, and he was tired of chasing kids who missed class or didn't do their homework.

First Steps

In 2013, Matthew attended a conference to, as he explained, "find out what those administrators are going to throw at us next, the new 'great idea,' so that I could help my teachers avoid all of it." With skepticism firmly in hand, he attended Jonathan's first session at the conference—and then never left the room. Matthew stayed for all four of Jonathan's sessions because he realized that flipped learning might not only solve his problem of students who missed class; it might truly change everything. He was intrigued and determined to try.

Back at his school, Matthew started rudimentarily flipping with his algebra classes. These were his "middle of the road" students, and he wanted to see if flipping would work. During the first few months, he spent time working out a lot of the technical and logistical aspects of flipped learning: how to make a video, how to give access to students, and how to ensure that students did the pre-work. But what surprised him was that he was grossly underprepared for what he should do with class time. When he was a traditional teacher, he spent so much time lecturing that when he flipped his instruction, he didn't know what to do with the extra time. At first, he used the extra time to teach students more content. But when he asked for feedback from students, they felt that the frenetic pace of his class was overwhelming.

When Matthew rolled into his first full year of flipped teaching, he expanded it to include more classes. He also took a new approach to his extra time: He began to explore project-based learning and more peer-to-peer interaction. He realized that one of the critical benefits of flipped learning was that his students were able to be so much more interactive in their learning. His classroom became filled with whiteboards on which his students were constantly engaged in doing math in collaborative groups. No longer were they sitting in chairs and listening; instead, they were actively and interactively learning together.

As Matthew continued to flip his classes, he found it solved his "kids missing class problem." Then it solved his reteaching problem. Then flipped learning solved his record-keeping problem. And over the course of a few years, his whole mindset of what school should look like changed. He started out as a very traditional and somewhat successful teacher. Over time, he became an innovative educator.

Sharing Innovation

Flipped learning then provided Matthew with some amazing opportunities. He had kept in contact with Jonathan, who encouraged him to take a more significant role in the flipped learning community. Matthew began to lead professional development for teachers. He started writing blog posts and eventually published a book. He became active on the Flipped Learning Network (an organization we founded as a place for educators to connect and learn about flipping), and he is now chairman of the board of the Flipped Learning Network. All this from a guy who came to a conference to learn how to stop the "next thing."

When the COVID-19 pandemic hit, Matthew was better prepared than almost every other teacher in his school. In fact, the school asked him to help other teachers as they moved to remote learning. However, this led to frustration because his administration was neither willing to see nor support the best practices of flipped learning.

During the summer of 2020, Matt was contacted by a neighboring school district that wanted him because of his expertise in flipped learning, and he jumped at the opportunity. He is now happily back teaching students and inspiring them to reach heights he could have never imagined when he was teaching traditionally.

Looking to the Future

Matthew continues to think about the implications of flipped classrooms in a post-pandemic world. During the pandemic, all teachers learned both how to put content online and to post videos for instruction. But Matthew is concerned that since many teachers didn't implement best practices of flipped learning in their classrooms, many students are burned out with video. He doesn't have all the answers for what is next, but he is optimistic that as more teachers learn the best practices of flipped learning, students and teachers will see the profound value of flipped classrooms across the globe.

When we asked him what his biggest issue was in making the shift to flipped learning, he answered, "changing my mindset." Changing the mindset and direction of a whole school is even harder, but it can be done. And the results can be spectacular, as our next case study demonstrates.

Ashhurst Primary School, Ashhurst, New Zealand

In 2016, Heath Chittenden was named principal at the Ashhurst Primary School and was in search of answers. The students, especially the boys, at his small school in semi-rural New Zealand were struggling to meet national academic standards. Their achievement was especially low in writing, and he was also looking for ways to challenge his staff to take their school to the next level.

Ashhurst Primary School had received the gold standard from the New Zealand Department of Education and was by all rights considered a top school. But Heath knew that they could do so much more. As a new principal, he saw a lot of teacher talk and not a lot of engaged students. He described his students as compliant and dutiful. "There was lots of huey, and not a lot of doey" at his school, Heath explained, calling on a New Zealand saying. In other words, there were a lot of outward signs of success but not as much real education happening. He could have rested on his laurels and kept things the same way, but he knew there was so much that his school could become.

In search of ideas, Heath flew to the 2016 ISTE conference in Denver. Having previously heard Jonathan speak about how flipping classes could transform schools, he decided to attend our joint session on the topic in Denver to refresh his memory. This time when he returned home, Heath couldn't get flipped learning out of his mind. Heath was so convinced about the efficacy of flipped learning that he reached out to Jonathan and invited him to present to the Ashhurst Primary staff. Because he wanted his staff to make the idea of flipped learning their own, however, Heath didn't tell them how vested he was. Instead, he told them only that he'd seen Jonathan speak at a conference and that he wanted them to "hear what this guy has to say and see if his ideas would have any merit here at Ashhurst." Only his senior staff knew how much he wanted the school to embrace flipped learning.

Jonathan vividly remembers the visit to Ashhurst. His drive from Wellington took him through idyllic New Zealand sheep country and past a beautiful series of water features. He also remembers meeting a reticent staff upon his arrival. Over the course of two days, however, Jonathan talked about the transformational nature of flipped learning, the contents of this book, and the flipped classrooms he had been seeing around the world. He spoke to them as a fellow teacher who had found a better way to reach every student, and the staff warmed to his message. That two-day workshop proved to be the spark for an amazing and still continuing story—the story of a school transformed by flipped learning.

From Idea to Implementation

Once the teachers were convinced, the hard work began. It's one thing to love the *idea* of flipping a class and another thing to *actually* flip a class. Additionally, it's one thing to flip a *class* and a whole different animal to flip an entire *school*. Ashhurst Primary's journey was one of incremental changes and a lot of hard work, with all teachers and leaders working together toward one goal: to reach their students.

The journey started with a handful of selected Ashhurst teachers flipping a few units for the remainder of that first school year. Their purpose was to find out what software worked, where to post flipped videos, the best way for students to access the digital content, and what logistical challenges they needed to overcome. Although the school was a 1:1 device school, quite a few technical challenges still needed to be addressed.

The next year, all teachers were expected to flip the writing portion of their classes. To get everybody ready, Ashhurst teachers took a flipped learning certification course that Jonathan created. This course gave them a common language and common strategies to incorporate into their classes.

The journey was not without roadblocks. Some teachers made videos that were too long, so the school implemented a rule that videos couldn't be longer than three minutes. They found that it was critical to create their own video content, rather than rely on content created by others and posted on YouTube. Some teachers were great with videos but struggled to effectively use their extra time in class. Some even made great videos and then simply played them in class for all students to watch communally. Heath and his leadership team spent great amounts of time in teachers' classes and working one on one and in small groups, discussing and demonstrating the best practices of flipped learning.

During the second year of full implementation, Heath and his team expected all teachers to flip reading and math and continued to contextualize how flipped learning would work at Ashhurst. They found ways to share files and ways for teachers to share their work with each other. Recognizing that they were a Google school, for example, they decided to move everything to Google Drive. They also began to realize that students could go deeper into the course material. Using Bloom's Taxonomy to center on the quality of instruction, they aimed to get students to engage in more cognitively rigorous work. They tinkered with project-based learning and started using it as a means to facilitate deeper understanding.

Heath admits that the workload for the first two years was overwhelming. By the end of the second year, however, teachers were starting to see the results of all of their hard work. Students were more engaged, achievement was up, and they realized that once they created all of the pre-learning activities, the following years would be easier.

During the third year of implementation, they continued tweaking their processes. One problem they found was that a student who was behind in Year 4 (4th grade) might be watching a Year 2 (2nd grade) video made by a Year 2 teacher. That wasn't working, because the instruction made the Year 4 student feel belittled. So the Year 4 teachers stepped up and created content that taught the concepts with a voice that spoke to the students just where they were at.

The Journey to Mastery

But Ashhurst wasn't done. As their transformation continued, they began to see what they were doing as a journey toward mastery learning. They had already identified the key learning targets, and it was natural for them to become a flipped-mastery school. To be honest, it didn't look too much like what we described earlier in this book, but the school had fully embraced mastery learning nonetheless.

One example of their "all in" approach was when they realized that many students in their upper grades needed to learn specific techniques to take notes. Younger students would watch a flipped video to answer one or two questions. But older students needed to learn a way to process more information at once. So they began a unit in their Year 7 (7th grade) classes that taught students how to take notes. Mastering note-taking helped students to be better prepared for the high schools they would later attend.

By all measures, Ashhurst saw a remarkable improvement. Over the course of four years, writing achievement increased by 25%

for boys and 16% for all students. Math achievement went up by 13%. Since they were literally the first school to flip in all of New Zealand, accolades came as well. Ashhurst Primary became a model school where the teaching staff felt validated and empowered.

During the COVID-19 pandemic, they didn't miss a beat. While the achievement of many schools suffered, Ashhurst Primary School continued to improve on measures of learning. Staff heard from parents that they were so glad their kids were at Ashhurst instead of at other schools that were not prepared for remote learning. Shortly after the lockdowns, Heath received a record wave of applicants to teach at the school—at a time when the number of teachers was declining and many schools had difficulty finding enough teachers to fill their staff.

Spreading the Word

And their journey continues today. Ashhurst has very little staff turnover, but those teachers who do leave tend to become leaders at their new schools, spreading the word of flipped learning. Meanwhile, teachers flock to Ashhurst Primary School. Due to their success, it is common for other schools to send teachers to visit. Some of these visiting teachers are now teaching at Ashhurst. They see the system and the results, and they want to be there. Teachers report that they love being at Ashhurst because they are doing what really matters. They now spend less time planning than virtually all other schools, and yet they are more prepared than almost any other school due to all of the hard work the staff put in during the early years.

Rather than rest on its success with flipped learning, however, Ashhurst continues its quest to develop and refine. They found that they had gone too far into projects, for example, because students weren't engaging as deeply with the subject as they needed to. Their emphasis today is on questioning strategies that will ensure that all students learn deeply.

Common Threads

As we have traveled the world since the publication of the first edition of this book, we have seen Matthew's and Ashhurst Primary School's stories repeated over and over again. Jonathan remembers talking to a South Korean teacher who was in tears while describing how flipped learning changed her life. When she shared flipped learning with her traditional teacher father, his career was revitalized. We remember tutoring a teacher in Missouri's Ferguson-Florissant School District, which used flipped learning while schools were closed due to protest riots over the shooting of an unarmed Black man. We chatted with a teacher in Iran who transformed his school through flipped learning. We visited a flipped school in Birmingham, England, where the day before our visit there was a gang-related death. The school was a beacon of hope in the midst of their world, and school leaders attributed their success to flipped learning. Jonathan spoke with the minister of education for Jordan as he wondered how he would meet the educational needs of the refugees flooding his country. At the onset of the Russia-Ukraine war, we had a chance to work with an international school that had been forced online due to the conflict.

We have seen flipped learning work in exclusive private schools and in economically depressed schools. We have seen it work in elementary schools, middle schools, high schools, universities, and in the corporate world. We have consulted with schools of all stripes and varieties. We have met with secretaries of education and helped a province in Argentina flip its entire educational system. We have met with ambassadors and worked with Fortune 100 companies. All of the success of the model has been overwhelming at times. We were just a couple of teachers in little Woodland Park, Colorado, who wanted to help our students. We had no idea the impact the model nor this book would have upon the world. And the model still works! If you haven't implemented flipped learning yet, *try*. It isn't too late.

conclusion

Although we know that the lecture is not the best means of communicating information to students, sometimes direct instruction has a place. That place, however, is not in the classroom and not in a whole-class setting. We have also learned that delivering instruction with a video can be very effective for some topics, but not as effective for others. Some concepts must be discovered independently by a student, others are best taught directly, and still others under a Socratic dialogue. Our videos are not the end-all of education, but they have allowed us to better explore models of education that are best for our students. We encourage you to explore and hybridize what you have learned from this book, adapting it to what you already know to be good teaching practice.

 Reversing the traditional lecture and homework elements of my class and integrating engaged-learning activities transitioned my course from a teacher-centered to a learner-centered environment. This completely changed the dynamics of the classroom and made students more responsible for their own learning. Student attendance, engagement, participation, and conceptual understanding all sharply increased and resulted in vastly improved student learning outcomes."

—Erik N. Christensen, College Physics Professor,
South Florida State College, Avon Park, FL

Developing what has grown to be known as the flipped classroom has been quite a journey for both of us. We are humbled by the explosion and global spread of something that started in two classrooms in rural Colorado and a few other scattered places.

We were simply a couple of teachers who wanted to do what was best for students and jumped in. We didn't realize the implications of what we had stumbled on. Now, however, we realize that the flipped and flipped-mastery models have the potential to make a positive impact on education.

We also want to acknowledge all the educators and students who have grown with us through this process and have influenced our thinking about the flipped classroom. This book shares our story from our perspective, and we know that many other amazing educators have been using these same tools, skills, and resources for years. We can only hope that the wisdom and experience of others continues to shape the flipped classroom. So much of what we practice on a daily basis was inspired by other teachers using similar instructional tools and then adapted to meet our needs. We don't claim to have invented some new pedagogy, and we have not tried to brand an innovation. We simply saw a need and met it with an available technological tool—and were so excited with the results that we felt compelled to tell the world.

If you are considering flipping your classroom, we want you to be sure you're doing it for the right reasons. One of the hardest things we had to do when switching to the flipped model (and ultimately the flipped-mastery model) was to give control of the learning over to the students. For many educators, this is very difficult. But when learning is in the hands of the students and not in the hands of the teacher, real learning occurs. Strong constructivists and die-hard project-based learning advocates will say that we haven't gone far enough in handing over the learning to our students. They may be right. However, flipping the classroom is an easy step that any teacher can take to move away from in-class direct instruction to more student-directed and inquiry-based learning.

As we share our story around the country, we hear over and over from teachers, administrators, parents, and most importantly students how much they want the flipped model implemented.

Teachers who went into education to help kids see the model as a way to achieve their ultimate goal of teaching. Administrators like the fact that flipping the classroom is scalable, reproducible, and customizable and doesn't require a great deal of money. Parents love the model because they see it as a way for their children to learn deeply instead of just being exposed to information. And last, and most important, students appreciate the model for so many reasons: It speaks their language, it teaches them to take responsibility for their own learning, it is flexible,

 The flipped classroom was supposed to solve a problem in my classroom, instead it highlighted that my completely teacher-driven, homework-focused classroom was the problem. Flipped learning was the door to reflection, revision, and refocus that put the focus on student learning and reignited my passion for teaching."

—Matthew Moore, High School Math Teacher,
Warrensburg-Latham High School, Warrensburg, IL

and it allows them to work at the pace that works best for them.

We both believe that good teaching happens in the context of healthy student–teacher relationships. Students need to see adults as mentors and guides instead of experts from on high. Teachers need to see students not as helpless kids who need to be spoon-fed their education, but rather as unique individuals who require a unique education. The flipped and flipped-mastery models have allowed us to empower students to want to learn more content more deeply in an interactive, relationship-rich environment that helps them succeed.

Now we charge you, our reader, with the challenge to go out and do whatever it takes to think differently about education. Though you may not adopt our models fully, we encourage you to ask one question: "What is best for kids?" Then go and do it.

APPENDIX **A**

best practices for
making quality
educational videos

One of the most common questions we hear is "Should I develop my own flipped activities, or is it okay to use online lessons?" This is frequently followed by the sentiment "I'm not super comfortable creating videos" or "I don't have the time." We understand these concerns; making your own videos takes significant time, energy, and creativity. At the same time, we have worked with countless teachers across the world, and those who create most of their own content are more successful flipped class teachers. The goal of the tips and suggestions that follow is to make you more successful too.

The Value of Creating Your Own Content

The primary reason that creating your own flipped videos is the best practice is that doing so enhances the student–teacher relationship. Students who see you on the video see the time and passion you put into your class, as well as find a greater sense of connection to you and to the content you are presenting. Students also see you as the expert on the subject and this adds to your credibility. Creating your own content can also dispel the common myth students in a flipped class often pass to their parents: "My teacher is not teaching anymore." If you use only flipped videos you found online, the student has a point. But when you create your own, this is demonstrably not true.

Hear us carefully. You can flip using other teachers' content, but when you start to make your own, you will be using the best practices we have seen repeated in thousands of classrooms across the world. Yes, it takes time. Yes, you may have to learn new skills and technology. But, yes again, it is worth that effort. And we're here to help. Let's start with a few of the key principles to apply when creating your flipped videos.

Building Quality Learning Objects

We don't recommend that you produce sub-par learning objects. Almost all the teachers we interact with tell us that simply having a PowerPoint slideshow loaded onto a site is insufficient. People expect more. In a culture of high-gloss digital media and short attention spans, students need a brief but compelling experience in which they can connect to both the content and a person. Most teachers find video to often be the best way to meet the learning goals. But don't obsess about making the perfect flipped video. Creating lots of good videos is better than polishing one or two that are "perfect."

Length of Flipped Videos

In a typical face-to-face class where the teacher "teaches," the presentation of material often can be long and protracted. We have all sat through a boring, seemingly endless PowerPoint presentation. When implementing a flipped model, it is important to keep the learning objects short and focused.

We continually hear from teachers that they think there is no way they can compress the content of a 45-minute face-to-face class into a short video. After training thousands of teachers in flipped methodologies, we have learned that it can be done. Typically, teachers' first videos are about half the length of their face-to-face presentations, and with practice, we have seen most teachers cut the ratio to one third. Our videos started out at 15–25 minutes, and as we honed our craft of video production, we were able to get the content down to 8–12 minutes. And if the content students need is greater, we recommend that you break the subject up into smaller, bite-sized pieces. A general guideline we recommend is one minute per grade level of the students. So, if you are teaching seventh grade, aim for a 7-minute video.

Building In Interactivity

It is not simply good enough to create videos that will be passively watched. Instead, try to build interactivity into them. The goal is for students to interact with the content, which then sets them up for a more engaging face-to-face experience.

Teaching Students How to Watch Flipped Videos

Watching an instructional video is different than watching a video for entertainment. Students inherently understand how to watch the latest superhero film, but they often need to be taught how to watch instructional content. We liken the difference to learning to read a textbook rather than a novel: It is a skill that must be taught. Spend a little time in the introduction to your course teaching students how to interact with the content.

One technique that has worked for us is a three-step model in which students watch the video twice and answer questions at the end:

Step 1: Watch, listen, and process. Students watch, listen, and process the information on the video. They are encouraged not to take notes, but to watch and absorb.

Step 2: Pause and write. Students write down what they've seen in the video. This ensures that they have another opportunity to process what they've just seen as they transcribe the video. Also, they now have a record of their learning to refer to during practice in the face-to-face class time.

Step 3: Demonstrate accountability. Students answer a few questions after the video is done. This is typically done in the school's learning management system and provides context and information for increasing the value of class time.

Following are some techniques you can use to increase inter-action. Some of the tools are low-tech, requiring no fancy technological tools except pencil and paper, and some are more advanced digital tools which track and measure student engagement.

Organizers. This could be as simple as a fill in the blank "guided notes sheet," a template, a binder with questions, or a page with all the necessary charts and problems. Some teachers will even place a QR code on the handout that will take students directly to the associated flipped video.

3-2-1 strategy. In this strategy, students record three things they learned from the video, two questions about the content of the video, and one lingering question they still have. During class students report the three things they learned, interact with each other about the two questions, and share with the teacher the one thing they did not understand. And if students feel they grasped the content, they list a takeaway that summarizes their learning.

Assessment tools. There are many ways to acquire direct student feedback from a flipped video. Tools such as Google Forms, online assessment suites, and most learning management systems have quizzing features which allow you to get immediate feedback on learning.

Assessment tools in the videos. Many online services contain tools that can insert questions within the flipped video. The video will pause and ask each student to respond to a question or prompt. Teachers have access to analytics that tell them who watched the video, how long each student watched the video, and which ques-tions they answered correctly. These services can also provide discussion forums about the video. One tool we like is Edpuzzle (edpuzzle.com). There are also a host of enterprise-level video hosting platforms that allow for built-in interactions inside of the videos, such as TechSmith's products (techsmith.com/lecture-capture.html),

VidGrid (vidgrid.com), and Panopto (panopto.com) to name a few.

There is no one way to build in interactivity. And there is no one tool which is best for every teacher. Finding what works best in any class depends on many factors, and each teacher must find the right mix of interactive techniques, tools, and systems.

Principles of Good Digital Design

Richard Mayer did extensive research on how people learn best when presented with multimedia and summarized his findings in the following twelve principles (Mayer, 2021). Although we're applying these principles to flipped videos (our italicized comments follow Mayer's definitions), they apply to any multimedia-based content for learning.

1. **Coherence Principle:** People learn better when extraneous words, pictures, and sounds are excluded rather than included. Keep your pre-learning videos/texts simple and focused. *Too much detail can detract from learning. You don't want to overload learners.*

2. **Signaling Principle:** People learn better when cues that highlight the organization of the essential material are added. *Provide organizers in advance so that students can clearly follow along with the flipped video.*

3. **Redundancy Principle:** People learn better from graphics and narration than from graphics, narration, and on-screen text. *If you simply read text that is already on the screen, learning decreases.*

4. **Spatial Contiguity Principle:** People learn better when corresponding words and pictures are presented near rather than far from each other on the page or screen. *Make sure related text and graphics appear near each other on the screen.*

5. **Temporal Contiguity Principle:** People learn better when corresponding words and pictures are presented simultaneously rather than successively. If you use a voiceover, synchronize it with what is happening on the screen. *Avoid a lag between words and pictures.*

6. **Segmenting Principle:** People learn better from a multimedia lesson that is presented in user-paced segments rather than as a continuous unit. *Keep your videos short.*

7. **Pre-training Principle:** People learn better from a multimedia lesson when they know the names and characteristics of the main concepts. *If new terms are being introduced, the flipped video will be more effective if learners have a "cheat sheet" to refer to.*

8. **Modality Principle:** People learn better from graphics and narrations than from animation and on-screen text. *Narration is better than having large amounts of text on the screen—no matter how creatively the text is presented.*

9. **Multimedia Principle:** People learn better from words and pictures than from words alone. *Add brief text annotations to any images in your flipped videos.*

10. **Personalization Principle:** People learn better from multimedia lessons when words are in conversational style rather than formal style. *Don't be stiff. Be yourself.*

11. **Voice Principle:** People learn better when the narration in multimedia lessons is spoken in a friendly human voice rather than a machine voice. *Don't rely on text-to-speech software. Invest in a good microphone and narrate the video yourself.*

12. **Image Principle:** People do not necessarily learn better from a multimedia lesson when the speaker's image is added to the screen. *We like to include our images in our videos, but it is not absolutely necessary for you to be on the screen in yours.*

Following Mayer's lead, we created our own list of good design principles when we first pioneered flipped learning in the K–12 space. Following is our list of the top twelve tips you should keep in mind when creating flipped videos.

1. **Keep videos short.** We are teaching the YouTube generation, and they want things in bite-sized pieces. If you're teaching the quadratic formula, teach just the quadratic formula. Don't teach anything else. While it's tempting to simply re-create your lectures in your videos, remember to stay focused: One topic equals one video. With this in mind, we try to keep our videos under 15 minutes at most and under 10 minutes at best. We have also found that the general guideline of "one minute per grade level" is a good rule of thumb. For example, if you are teaching eighth grade, aim for 8 minutes.

2. **Animate your voice.** When you are making these videos, you may be using some sort of slide presentation software. The only things you have to engage your students besides your slides are your pen and your voice. Change the inflection of your voice. Make the videos exciting. If you choose to make your videos live in front of students, your inflection will be more natural. However, if you're talking to a computer, it is especially important to animate your voice and make it interesting. For example, Jonathan occasionally jumps into a mixture of a Russian/German/French/Italian/Scottish/indiscernible-dialect accent. Some students find this amusing, and they never know when he might mix it up for them. As we got more proficient with the software, we were able to relax and be ourselves more and more in front of a computer. You, too, will get better as you make more and more videos. Your first ones will not be very good, but as you continue, you will improve. Embrace the learning process.

3. **Work with a partner.** There is something powerful about watching two people having a conversation instead of watching one person talk. Think about your morning commute. When was the last time you heard only one voice on the radio? Stations realize that a conversation is far more engaging than a single talking head. Our students told us the same thing. Two heads (and voices) are better than one. Students learn more. Because we've both been teaching for quite some time, we know which topics students will typically struggle with, so one of us usually takes on the role of the student learning the material while the other takes on the role of an expert. Students tell us this dialogue is helpful in their comprehension of the material.

   Working with a partner was also a great way to introduce other teachers to the flipped classroom. Jonathan started teaching his freshmen using the flipped-mastery model in 2009 and did it all alone. The next year, our whole team of freshman science teachers followed the model. At first the team used Jonathan's videos, but then he began working with each teacher to create their own. Jonathan ran the technology while the other teacher acted as the expert, enabling them to ease into the video production process. Some were reluctant to embrace the flipped model because they were intimidated by the technology required. After working with Jonathan, they realized that they were simply having a conversation, which was recorded for their students.

4. **Add appropriate humor.** We typically have some sort of a running joke in our videos. We usually do this for the first minute of each video. Students either love these or hate them. Because they know the joke will take up only the first minute, those who like our weird sense of humor tune in, and those who don't just fast forward. In one iteration of our videos we had the running joke of Jonathan trying to figure out which instrument he

should play. Invariably, he was poor at almost all he tried, until he eventually found the harmonica and played it quite well. Things like this bring interest and a certain wackiness to the videos, which helps keep the students interested. If you have running jokes or themes in your classroom, incorporate those into your videos as well.

5. **Audio matters.** If you are recording your video, make sure your audio is clean and understandable. It may seem counterintuitive, but good audio is more important than good video in a video. Invest in a decent microphone, and use your teacher voice. If your students can't make out what you're saying, how can they learn?

6. **Don't waste your students' time.** We've watched teacher-made videos where teachers talk about their favorite football team for five minutes. Students are watching on their own time, and this sort of tangent wastes it. Keep to your topic.

7. **Use less text, more pictures.** Since many lectures start as a PowerPoint deck, many teachers tend to simply go through their text-heavy slides. Video is a visual medium; pictures are more important than text. Err on the side of more pictures. The text should be the script that you read, and the slides should be simple and clean.

8. **Annotate.** Think of your screen as a whiteboard with cool pictures. Use annotation equipment to add pen markups. We don't think we would ever have embraced the flipped classroom if the annotation feature had not been available. Because we primarily teach chemistry, we need some sort of a digital chalkboard to write on. Solving complex chemical problems has always involved writing. Having a way to digitally write on the screen, at least for us, allowed the flipped classroom to become a reality.

9. **Enhance with video clips.** If your primary method of creation is a screencast, then splice in video clips of other interesting or relevant material. For example, add a video clip of a teacher showing how to check someone's pulse in a video about the circulatory system.

10. **Be present with picture-in-picture.** People like to know who they are learning from. Many software tools can add a teacher's webcam feed onto a screencast. Personalizing the learning in this way makes the flipped video more authentic. (This may seem like a contradiction to Mayer's Image Principle, but his research applied to only a static image of the teacher appearing in the multimedia).

11. **Ask questions.** Use some sort of technology tool to add questions into the flipped video. These questions can happen inside of the flipped video or could be placed at the end.

12. **Keep it copyright friendly.** Because these videos will likely be posted online, make sure that you follow all appropriate copyright laws. Use pictures that you have taken or that are in the public domain, use royalty-free music, and avoid copying and pasting from your textbooks unless you either have permission to do so or keep the videos off publicly viewable channels. Give credit where credit is due with proper citation or Creative Commons license. We are not copyright lawyers, nor do we play one on TV. Please consult experts (probably your librarian or media specialist) in this area to ensure that you don't infringe on the copyrights of others.

ISTE STANDARD IN ACTION

Leader (2.2.b)

One of the most beautiful things about using technology to create flipped classrooms is the ability to give equitable access to the content. Our students don't all learn the same way or at the same speed. Some students have processing difficulties, hearing impairments, or language barriers. Utilizing technology to flip your lessons, whether that is through video, slideshows, audio or video on slideshows, etc., allows students to access content in a way that works best for them. I always use video creation software that allows the creation of subtitles, whether they are created automatically, like with YouTube, Screencastify, WeVideo Classroom, Canvas Studio, or Microsoft Flip, or created manually with other video-creation software. This is an accessibility feature that should be offered to all students and can often be set to translate in different languages.

Giving all students access to content in a flipped manner also allows students to review the content, replay, pause, and process, all on their own time. I model how I interact with digital content for students in small groups, pausing the video or reading and explaining how I process and think out loud. Students might not use all of the strategies I offer, but being able to use them privately if necessary is a huge benefit for everyone, and adds another tool in their toolbelt to use in all aspects of their lives.

—MORIAH WALKER, CYBERSECURITY EDUCATOR, LAKOTA LOCAL
SCHOOLS, LIBERTY TOWNSHIP, OH

Ways to Create a Flipped Video

When people think of flipped learning, they think about students watching videos at home. And though flipped learning is *not* primarily about the videos, most people *do* use video in flipped classrooms—and there the similarities diverge. In our travels we've seen teachers use a variety of methods to create flipped videos. So, if you're not comfortable talking to a lens, you have options!

Simple Video

Video shot from a camera or mobile device can be a highly effective tool. Virtually everyone knows how to shoot videos with their smartphone, and videos created in this way are especially good at demonstrating a skill or process. We know one pottery teacher who creates flipped videos about the various ways to use a pottery wheel. Another teacher creates cooking videos for his food course. Another teacher sets up her smartphone on a tripod while she teaches math at a whiteboard.

Screencasting

By far, the most common way teachers create video for flipped learning is via a screencast. Screencasting programs record whatever is happening on your computer screen along with audio, and in some cases, a webcam feed. Teachers typically create a lesson or presentation in Microsoft PowerPoint or a similar app, and then use a screencasting program to record them teaching through their slide deck. You can even digitally draw over the slides as you teach to enhance the production quality. If your content requires some sort of software demonstration, screencasting is a must. Table A.1 offers a list of some screencasting programs you may want to check out; there's something for every operating system and device.

TABLE A.1 Recommended Screencasting Programs

Program	Platform	Description	Learn More
ScreenPal	Windows, macOS	Web-based screen recording tool	
Snagit	Windows, macOS	A tool for screen capture and image or short video editing	

Program	Platform	Description	Learn More
Camtasia	Windows, macOS	Premium screencasting and editing software	
Screencastify	Windows, macOS	Screencasting plugin for Chrome browser	
ScreenFlow	macOS	Premium screencasting software for Mac	
Explain Everything	Android, iPadOS, iOS	iPad video creation tool	
TouchCast	iPadOS	iPad video creation tool that adds VR elements	
ShowMe	iPadOS, iOS	Video creation and delivery system	
Doceri	Windows, iPadOS	Whiteboard video recording tool	
Educreations Interactive Whiteboard	iPadOS	Interactive whiteboard and screencasting tool	

ISTE STANDARD IN ACTION

Leader (2.2.a)

Creating videos via screencasting software has been a beneficial tool to lead students in step-by-step instructional videos. Often, students are more apt to be comfortable with these technologies than their teachers. Many students, especially early finishers, enjoy helping create how-to videos for me to use in my training sessions. This includes simple tasks such as adding new fonts to Google Docs or changing their theme in the Chrome browser. Students get a kick out of the idea that they make videos that are used to train other students or even teachers! Allowing the students to make simple how-to videos takes the pressure off of me, gives me more time, and gives them a chance to be a part of the learning process for everyone in the classroom (and beyond). Even though the how-to videos are simple and may not feel like something we need to spend time on, they are real-life skills that I get asked for often. Being able to send a video of a student explaining how to complete a task accomplishes many tasks at once.

—LANCY COLLINS, INSTRUCTIONAL COACH FOR TECHNOLOGY, PK–12, HOMER CENTRAL SCHOOLS, HOMER, NY

Lightboards

If you frequently use a whiteboard but prefer to face your students while teaching, consider using a lightboard. A lightboard is a piece of glass on which you can draw to highlight specific content. Because it's glass, you can see through the board to your students (and the camera) on the other side and they can see you while you demonstrate concepts. With more powerful editing software, you can overlay images and videos onto the board's video. Many schools have accelerated their flipped classroom rollout by building or purchasing their own lightboard studio. You can learn more about lightboards at lightboard.info, revolutionlightboards.com, or learning.glass.

Document Cameras

Many schools have document cameras that project a flat image on the screen, but did you realize that these cameras also have the ability to record video? This usually works when the camera is plugged into a computer via a USB hub. Some of the newer document cameras can record without being connected to a computer, saving their video files to an SD card.

Animation Videos

You have all seen the cool video clips in which someone draws quickly on-screen accompanied by a voiceover. This is done a lot in advertising. After all, nowhere is the pressure to be extremely engaging in a short period of time greater than in ads. These videos are engaging and can be very effective. To easily create your own animations, check out Powtoon (powtoon.com), VideoScribe (videoscribe.co), and Moovly (moovly.com).

Augmented Reality

The emergence of games such as Pokemon GO demonstrated the viability of augmented reality. Many flipped class teachers are now creating some flipped videos using augmented reality. With a Merge Cube (mergeedu.com/cube) and an app on your smartphone, for example, you can display a 3D hologram of a human brain in your hand and describe the parts. This can be converted into a video that students can watch as their flipped video.

Adding Questions to Your Videos

One way to make your flipped videos interactive and active is to have students respond to prompts and questions about the video. This gives you valuable feedback that adds accountability for students, helps you know what students comprehend, and informs your instruction.

The Value of Questions

You can sprinkle questions throughout the video or place them at the very end. Which is the most effective approach? It turns out that the placement doesn't matter as much as the presence of questions.

A study by psychologist Dr. Henry Roediger of Washington University in St. Louis (2007) compared the effect of questions in a flipped video using three groups:

- Group One watched a video with no questions asked.

- Group Two watched a video with questions interspersed throughout. The video paused at the questions for students to answer.

- Group Three watched a video with questions at the end.

When the students were tested six weeks later, there was little difference between those who answered interspersed questions and those who answered questions at the end of the video. Those who watched videos without questions at all, however, scored significantly lower on total retention. The obvious point is that questions add great value to the learning process.

The Type of Questions

When putting questions into a flipped video, another challenge many teachers encounter is determining the level of difficulty for the questions. Generally, knowledge and understanding questions vis-à-vis Bloom's Taxonomy (Bloom, 1956) are best. This allows students the ability to check for understanding and helps with critical recall. Using Bloom's Taxonomy as a guide is, in general, a good rule of thumb.

We suggest inserting an open-ended prompt toward the end of the video. Assuming the answer is submitted electronically, you can look over the responses and get a good feel for the level of student understanding and engagement on the topic. For example, you could ask:

- What do you not understand from this video?
- What are you curious about as a result of watching this video?
- Why do you think...?
- What do you predict will happen next with...?

Often, students ask questions in their response, which can reveal misconceptions and can both inform a better use of class time and also provide feedback for retooling the flipped video to make it clearer and more on point.

Pre-Video Questions

Shana K. Carpenter and Alexander Toftness from Iowa State University studied the effects of asking pre-questions prior to viewing video presentations (2017). They found that asking strategic questions that will help access prior knowledge and prepare students for learning significantly enhanced student learning. Steve Griffiths, a middle school science teacher in Queensland, Australia, has experimented with pre-questions and told us that ideal pre-questions either add a hook for the students or connect new content to knowledge students already know. He reports that he has seen improvement on students' answers to post-video questions because they have been doing the pre-questions.

Other Tools Besides Video

As we've said before, flipped learning is not about the videos. The heart of flipped learning is a reversal of how students interact with content on their own time versus in the classroom. With this in mind, there are many other mediums you can use. The question you should ask is: What is the best medium for presenting the "easy stuff," or, rather, the lower levels of Bloom's Taxonomy, to students?

Flipping with Text

Many teachers use text-based flipped content for students. Instead of assigning videos, Eric Mazur, a physics professor at Harvard University and early adopter of flipped learning, assigns readings to students and has them comment on the content online using the Perusall (perusall.com) platform. The tool, which the developer calls "an online social annotation platform," enables students to read each other's comments and then comment on them. The platform uses advanced machine language algorithms to analyze student comments and determine what students struggle with. When Eric prepares for class, he has the platform create a "confusion" report which then guides what happens during class.

Other options for flipping using text are the InsertLearning and Actively Learn platforms. InsertLearning (insertlearning.com) enables educators to build interactions into any webpage. You can add notes, questions, and discussions and then track student responses. ActivelyLearn (ActivelyLearn.com) enables you to add interactions to books, websites, and files. You can add questions, links, and comments, and then the tool provides detailed analytics of student interactions, such as how many minutes a student was reading the text and what interactions they did while using the tool.

Audio Files

Besides video- and text-based learning content, flipping with audio files can have a significant impact. One advantage of audio files is that they are more easily integrated into the daily life of students, who could listen during their ride from and to school, for example.

Ideal Time Between Prework and Classwork

In 2013, researchers at York and Santa Clara University asked university students to learn twenty Swahili-English word pairs (Bell et al., 2014). There were four groups:

- Group One learned the words and were given an immediate test afterward.

- Group Two learned the words in the morning and then took a memory test.

- Group Three learned the word pairs in the evening, had a night of sleep, and took a test 12 hours later.

- Group Four had 24 hours between learning and the test.

When the groups were tested, there was virtually no difference in their scores. However, the study went on to examine long-term retention and checked back with all participants after ten days. Those results were astounding. The longer the spacing between learning and testing, the greater the long-term retention. Remarkably, though, the difference between Groups Two and Three was also interesting in that although both of them had a 12-hour interval between learning and the test, the participants that had a sleep cycle between sessions performed better.

This study is one of many on the effect of sleep on long-term retention, and the implication is clear. It is best to have students exposed to the introductory material, sleep on it, and then practice it later if long-term retention and change are desirable.

APPENDIX B

we have answers (FAQs)

By now, we hope you have seen the benefit of the flipped classroom and have begun thinking about how to implement it in your setting. That means, of course, you probably have questions. What follows are answers to some questions we hear repeatedly in our travels, and we hope your burning inquiries are addressed here. We hope, too, you can learn from our mistakes.

Clearly there is more than one way to implement a flipped classroom, so what do all flipped classrooms have in common?

Believe it or not, not all flipped classrooms use videos as an instructional tool. A flipped classroom does not center around videos, but most teachers who flip use videos as a means of delivering direct instruction. The one unifying characteristic of all flipped classrooms is the desire to redirect the attention in a classroom away from the teacher and onto the learners and the learning. To do this, most flipped classroom teachers ask one question: What can I remove from my class time that does not require my physical presence and replace with something else that will be enhanced by my presence? Most (but not all) teachers who flip have answered this question with "lectures" or "direct instruction." Granted, you do not have to flip your class to turn the attention away from the teacher, and there are many valuable educational models and tools that help a teacher do so. A flipped classroom is one of those tools, but it is not the only tool available.

What about kids who don't watch the videos?

Because the vast majority of the direct instruction is delivered through videos, students who don't watch them are not prepared for class. In fact, non-viewing students will totally miss important content—just like if they skipped a traditional classroom's class. Our solution to this problem was relatively simple. In each of our classrooms we have two computers in the back of the room. Students who do not watch the videos at home are allowed to watch them in class. Students who have to use class time to watch the video miss out on the tutorial time, when the teacher walks around and helps students. Because all assignments are now done in class, these students have to complete their assignments at home as in a traditional model. Students quickly realize that it is to their benefit to have the teacher as a resource when working on their assignments, and most take the time to view the videos at home so they can take advantage of the time with the teacher. We find this to be a good motivator for the vast majority of our students.

Doesn't flipping increase homework time, especially if students watch videos for multiple classes?

In our case, the amount of time students spend viewing videos is approximately the same amount of time they used to spend doing homework. And in many cases, the time is reduced because in the traditional model, students who struggled with the content spent a much greater amount of time on the assignments they didn't understand. Our students who have more than one class with a video assignment don't report a greater amount of homework than before.

If your school has a no-homework culture or policy, you can still flip your class. However, you will have to design the class so that all the work (viewing videos, class work, assessment) could be done in class during school. This would most likely look like an asynchronous mastery class. Interestingly, some of our more efficient students have realized that they work quickly enough to complete all their work in our classes. These students don't do anything, including watching videos, outside of class.

Remember, a flipped class does not have to have videos, nor do the videos have to be viewed at home. The goal of flipping a classroom is to remove attention from the teacher and place it on the learner. If videos are to be used, and if they are to be viewed in class, then adequate and equitable access to appropriate technology *must* be in place before embarking on this endeavor. This should not dissuade the potential "flipper," but it must be addressed before moving in this direction. It would be unethical to create an educational environment in which some students could participate and others could not. By conscientiously dealing with equity issues before embarking on a flipped class, you can adopt the model no matter what your circumstances. As educators we must never dismiss a teaching tool simply because the potential for inequity exists. Just because a flipped classroom would not be appropriate in one setting does not mean it should not be adopted in another setting. We should think creatively, solve the problem at hand, and pursue what is best for our students. Inequity exists only because we let it exist. Create an equitable learning environment and proceed; if you cannot create an equitable environment, then don't flip.

How did you get your administration to buy in?

When we started flipping our classrooms, we just jumped in. We didn't get any preapproval from our administration. We just started. We had a great school with supportive administrators, and we always felt free to do what was best for kids. Shortly after we started flipping, our assistant superintendent came down to our classrooms and wanted to see what was happening. After seeing so many students engaged in learning, she invited us to share our model with our school board. Our message was well received by the board, and they fully supported the changes we were making because they saw how valuable it was for our students. In fact, when we told them about our challenges, they responded by updating our inadequate teacher computers.

You may wonder what challenges you might face when presenting the model to your administrators. We simply don't know. We were lucky, but we've heard a range of experiences from the teachers we've met and mentored. One, for example, first committed to flipping one instructional unit from her curriculum. She invited her principal to see the students learning, and after seeing how engaged the students were, the principal quickly gave her the green light to proceed. Others who have flipped tell us they had to go through a lengthy process of providing rationale and research that the model works.

How did you get parents to buy in?

We had a very supportive parent community. When we started flipping the classroom, the biggest concern was over access to the videos. Because we solved that problem, most parents were curious about the new approach. Once we explained the reason for the flip, most parents understood and were supportive. Each year during back-to-school night and in a letter to parents, we explain what the flip is and why we flipped. What we have found is that consistent, clear communication goes a long way when introducing something new. The flipped classroom is very different from what most parents experienced during their school years, but the vast majority of our students' parents have been appreciative.

Jonathan had one parent who initially expressed concern about the model. She thought that we were conducting an online class and that her daughter would not be interacting with her teacher on a regular basis. Once she fully understood the model, she emailed Jonathan and thanked him for actually *increasing* the interaction with her daughter. She noted that under the flipped classroom her daughter was able to access her teacher more easily than under a lecture model.

What do you do with students who do not buy in?

We wish we had a silver bullet to solve all the problems of education that exist today. However, we do not. Before we introduced the flipped classroom, we had roughly a 10% failure rate. With the flipped classroom, we had roughly a 10% failure rate, and under the flipped-mastery model, we had roughly a 10% failure rate. Unfortunately, we do not have an answer to this, and we have not been able to solve this issue. What we can say is this: Because we know our students better as a result of spending more time with each kid individually, we've noticed that each of our failing students has a story. Most of them have a difficult life situation, and school is simply not their priority. Knowing them better allows us to provide them the support they need.

One student in particular expressed great frustration with the flipped-mastery model and angrily cursed at Jonathan. After speaking with the student on a deeper level, we and his counselor were able to uncover some underlying problems in his life. Although he still failed the class, he was able to get the help he needed from the counselors. The flipped-mastery model is not directly responsible for this student receiving the help he needed, but it did let us know him much better than we would have in a traditional classroom and point him in a more positive direction.

Who makes the videos?

When we first started, we made all of the videos individually. Aaron would make unit 1 of Chemistry while Jonathan would make unit 1 of AP Chemistry. We would then flip which teacher did which class. As time went on and we made the second version of our videos (our first ones were not very good), we began to create them together. Making the videos together improved their quality significantly. The videos are now more of a conversation about science instead of the dissemination of scientific knowledge. As our videos began to receive some notoriety, we heard from teachers around the country that they were using our videos as supplements in their classrooms or, in some cases, as the primary means of instruction in their classes. It is okay to use someone else's videos! You don't have to make them all or all on your own. There is certainly value in students hearing their teacher's voice, reading their teacher's handwriting, and seeing their teacher's face on the instructional video. But to get started, you might consider using ready-made videos from other teachers. Then gradually make your own and phase the others out.

How do you find time to make the videos?

Because we had committed that first year to making *all* of our video lectures ahead of time, we somehow fit it all in. A morning person, Jonathan would often be at school before 6:00 a.m. making chemistry videos. Aaron, being the night owl, would put his kids to bed and then head to his laundry room to record videos. Somehow, we made it work. When we committed to doing the videos together, we would often come in before school or stay late to get them done. This certainly was a heavy time commitment—but worthwhile. Now that we've built a library of videos, we need only tweak and refine a few every year. Yes, creating your own videos will be hard and time-consuming at first, but we promise you it will be worth it. For your students' sake, make that commitment. You—and they—will be glad you did.

references

Akçayır, G., & Akçayır, M. (2018). The flipped classroom: A review of its advantages and challenges. *Computers & Education*, 126, 334–345. doi.org/10.1016/j. compedu.2018.07.021

Anderson, A., Franke, L., & Franke, W. (2017). Are your students flipping prepared? *Iowa State University Digital Repository.* dr.lib.iastate.edu/handle/20.500.12876/15587

Baker, J. W. (2016, June). The origins of "the classroom flip." *Proceedings of the 1st Annual Higher Education Flipped Learning Conference,* Greeley, Colorado.

Bell, M. C., Kawadri, N., Simone, P. M., & Wiseheart, M. (2014). Long-term memory, sleep, and the spacing effect, *Memory, 22*(3), 276–283. doi.org/10.1080/09658211. 2013.778294

Bergmann, J. (2022). *The mastery learning handbook: A competency-based approach to student achievement.* ASCD.

Bloom, B. S. (1956). *Taxonomy of educational objectives, handbook I: The cognitive domain.* David McKay Co Inc.

Bloom, B. S. (1971). Mastery learning. In J. H. Block (Ed.), *Mastery learning: Theory and practice* (pp. 47–63). Holt, Rinehart and Winston.

Carpenter, S. K., & Toftness, A. R. (2017). The effect of prequestions on learning from video presentations. *Journal of Applied Research in Memory and Cognition, 6*(1), 104–109.

CAST. (2018). *Universal Design for Learning Guidelines version 2.2.* udlguidelines.cast.org

Clayton Christensen Institute. (2023). *Blended learning models.* Blended Learning Universe. blendedlearning.org/models

Durak, H. Y. (2018). Flipped learning readiness in teaching programming in middle schools: Modelling its relation to various variables. *Journal of Computer Assisted Learning, 34*(6), 939–959. doi.org/10.1111/jcal.12302

Durak, H. Y. (2019). Examining the acceptance and use of online social networks by preservice teachers within the context of unified theory of acceptance and use of technology model. *Journal of Computing in Higher Education, 31,* 173–209. doi.org/10.1007/s12528-018-9200-6

Fu, M. Y. (2015, September 2). Medical school overhauls curriculum with major redesign. *The Harvard Crimson.* www.thecrimson.com/article/2015/9/2/hms-curriculum-major-revamp

Heo, H. J., & Chun, B. A. (2018). Improving the higher order thinking skills using flipped learning: Focused on the in-class activities with problem posing and solving. *Asia Life Sciences. 15*(4), 2187–2199.

Jantakoon, T., & Piriyasurawong, P. (2018). Flipped classroom instructional model with mobile learning based on constructivist learning theory to enhance critical thinking. *Journal of Theoretical and Applied Information Technology. 96*(16), 5607–5614.

Karpicke, J. D., & Roediger, H. L., III. (2007). Repeated retrieval during learning is the key to long-term retention. *Journal of Memory and Language, 57*(20), 151–162, doi.org/10.1016/j.jml.2006.09.004

Kim, E-J. (2020). A case study on the development and application of flipped learning based clinical dental hygiene curriculum. *Journal of Korean Society of Dental Hygiene, 20*(2), 155–166. doi.org/10.13065/jksdh.20200015

King, A. (1993). From sage on the stage to guide on the side. *College Teaching, 41*(1), 30–35.

Lage, M. J., Platt, G. J., & Treglia, M. (2000). Inverting the classroom: A gateway to creating an inclusive learning environment. *Journal of Economic Education, 31*(1), 30–43.

Malin, M. H., & Ginsberg, D. I. (2018). Flipping the classroom to teach workplace ADR in an intensive environment. *Journal of Legal Education. 67*(2), 615–625.

Mayer, R. E. (2021). Cognitive theory of multimedia learning. In R. E. Mayer & L. Fiorella (Eds.), *The Cambridge Handbook of Multimedia Learning* (3rd edition) (pp. 57–72). Cambridge University Press. doi.org/10.1017/9781108894333.008

Nielsen, P. L., Bean, N. W., & Larsen, R. A. A. (2018). The impact of a flipped classroom model of learning on a large undergraduate statistics class. *Statistics Education Research Journal, 17*(1), 121–140.

Pink, D. (2010, September 22). What a high school algebra teacher can teach us about innovation. *Daniel H. Pink.* www.danpink.com/2010/09/what-a-high-school-algebra-teacher-can-teach-us-about-innovation

Segumpan, L. L. B., & Tan, D. A. (2018). Mathematics performance and anxiety of junior high school students in a flipped classroom. *European Journal of Education Studies.* 4(12), 1–33. dx.doi.org/10.5281/zenodo.1325918

Talbert, R. (2015, January). Toward a common definition of "flipped learning." *The Chronicle of Higher Education*, 13–14.

Zhang, S. (2018). *A systematic review and meta-analysis on flipped learning in science education* [Thesis]. University of Hong Kong, Pokfulam, Hong Kong SAR.

index

Index